D0913868

The SWEET PEA Book

Graham Rice

Principal Photographer
judywhite/GardenPhotos.com

TIMBER PRESS
Portland, Oregon

Dedication

It was at my desk, in Pennsylvania, working on this book, that I heard the first plane had hit the World Trade Center. For some time afterwards, it was hard to write about sweet peas as we mourned for so many strangers, so needlessly dead, and sorrowed for the loved ones left behind to grieve.

But the book was finished and you have it in your hand. I will not presume to dedicate a mere gardening book to the memory of so many, so tragically lost. I simply urge you to use its advice to help you make your small part of the world more beautiful.

> ...Thou shalt remain, in midst of other woe
> Than ours, a friend to man, to whom thou say'st,
> 'Beauty is truth, truth beauty,' that is all
> Ye know on earth, and all ye need to know.

From "Ode on a Grecian Urn" by John Keats

© Graham Rice 2002
First published in the UK in 2002 by B T Batsford, London, UK

A member of **Chrysalis** Books plc

Paperback edition first published in North America in 2003 by Timber Press, Inc.

All photography © judywhite/GardenPhotos.com except where indicated on page 144. Title page picture 'Peacock'.

ISBN 0-88192-595-0

A CIP record for this book is available from the Library of Congress.

Printed in Singapore

Timber Press, Inc.
The Haseltine Building
133 S.W. Second Avenue, Suite 450
Portland, Oregon 97204, U.S.A.

www.timberpress.com

Contents

12/12/02 19.95

Introduction

This is a book for gardeners, for gardeners who grow sweet peas in beds and borders, tubs and even hanging baskets; for gardeners who sow a packet of mixed seed in the spring or dozens of individual varieties in the autumn; for gardeners who grow sweet peas for their fragrance and their colour and for cutting for the house.

Sweet peas are not difficult to grow. I will outline how to go about it with the least possible time and trouble, but to grow them well requires careful attention; this, also, I explain. Growing sweet peas up a clump of brushwood or a wigwam of bamboo canes is relatively straightforward and works well, but few gardeners integrate sweet peas into their border plantings or use them to create inspiring and attractive plant associations; I have many suggestions which I hope will provide inspirations in using these versatile flowers.

The explosion of interest in hanging baskets and other containers seems to have swept along without carrying the sweet pea in its wake, yet both traditional varieties and new types can be grown in containers: I will explain how and provide some enticing ideas for plant combinations.

Much of what has been written on sweet peas over the decades has been aimed at exhibitors, but these devotees are but a small minority of those enthusiastic growers for whom sweet peas are such a delight. Exhibitors have pioneered ways of growing sweet peas, researched their history, their peculiarities and their pests and diseases; they have raised many new varieties. Their contribution to sweet pea growing is enormous – but they are still a minority: in the United States they are practically non-existent. I discuss exhibiting, and breeding, sweet peas but my interest is more to help gardeners grow better sweet peas and use them more widely and more imaginatively in gardens.

Sweet peas were once the most widely grown of flowers; this may no longer be true, but these are exciting times in the sweet pea world. We have new dwarf sweet peas for hanging baskets, we have new varieties in the highly scented old-fashioned style, and we even have a revival in tall varieties without tendrils. There is also the possibility of a truly yellow sweet pea *on* the distant horizon, rather than far beyond it. Sweet peas are definitely back. Not as a show flower, but in gardens. It starts here.

Graham Rice

NOTES TO READERS

I have used the word variety, rather than cultivar, throughout in recognition of the fact that this is the term which most gardeners actually use for a cultivated variety. I apologize to those purists who may be offended by this affront to botanical correctness.

This book is written with both British and American readers in mind. Occasionally, there are remarks which may seem simplistic to readers in one country but which are helpful to those in the other and I would ask that readers not be irritated by this attempt to please all the readers all of the time.

The flowers in the studio photographs came from plants grown at Unwins Seeds near Cambridge, the Royal Horticultural Society's Garden at Wisley, Surrey and Sweet Pea Gardens, Surrey; our thanks go to all. Flowers also came from my own garden.

Chapter One
From the wild to our gardens

The native habitat of the wild sweet pea, *Lathyrus odoratus*, and its earliest introduction into the gardens of Western Europe, is a surprisingly contentious issue, provoking wildly contrasting opinions even today. Sweet peas have been taken all over the world, the robustness of their seeds having certainly been a help; whatever varieties are taken and grown, when they escape into a suitable climate they eventually revert to something approaching a wild type. This causes confusion.

Sicily, China, Malta, Sri Lanka – all have been suggested as the wild home of the sweet pea. But there is one aspect of the historical story on which most people now agree: in 1695 Francisco Cupani recorded the sweet pea as newly seen in Sicily. Cupani was a member of the order of St Francis, but he may not actually have been a monk as we have always assumed. He was in charge of the botanical garden at Misilmeri (15km/9 miles from Palermo) in Sicily and it is assumed that his garden was attached to the monastery although it is not entirely clear if his sweet pea was actually growing in the garden or wild in the surrounding area. In 1696, before Linnaeus simplified plant nomenclature, Cupani published a written description of the plant which he called *Lathyrus distoplatyphylos, hirsutus, mollis, magno et peramoeno, flore odoro*.

In 1699 he sent seed to Dr Casper Commelin, a botanist at the School of Medicine in Amsterdam, who included what is the first illustration of the plant in his account of the plants at the School published in 1701 where he records that the seeds came from Cupani. While there is no concrete contemporary evidence, it also seems clear that Cupani sent seed to Dr Robert Uvedale at the same time.

Dr Uvedale was a teacher who lived at Enfield in Middlesex and was a noted enthusiast for new and unusual plants; he enjoyed a very wide circle of notable friends and his was a well-known and much-visited garden. The first evidence of the plant being grown by Uvedale comes in 1700 on a herbarium specimen made by Dr Leonard Plukenet now at the British Museum (Natural History) in London. A note on the specimen refers to it having been collected from Uvedale's garden. British botanical pioneer John Ray also picked up on this new introduction, describing it in his *Historia Plantarum* of 1704 as: "Lathyrus major e Siciliae; a very sweet-scented Sicilian flower with a red standard; the lip-like petals surrounding the keel are pale blue."

So, Cupani noticed the sweet pea, his being the first printed reference. He definitely sent seed to Commelin and it seems most likely that he also sent seed to Uvedale. So far, so good.

There has long been a theory that sweet peas originated in Sri Lanka (Ceylon). In 1753 Linnaeus uses the name *Lathyrus zeylandicus* for a pink and white-flowered species supposedly originating in that country and this, with other red herrings, led the great authority Bernard Jones to believe as late as 1986 that sweet peas did, indeed, originate there. A much-respected earlier authority, E. R. Janes, held a similar conviction in 1953.

This opinion was fostered by Cornell University which, in 1897, in one of a series of otherwise excellent publications on sweet peas, asserted that Cupani himself had brought the pink and white pea from Ceylon to Italy. There are no wild sweet peas in Sri Lanka and this is confirmed by the *Flora of Ceylon* published in 1980.

Malta has also been suggested as a location for the wild home of the sweet pea, and one still propounded by Charles W. J. Unwin in the most recent edition of his classic *Sweet Peas: Their History, Development, Culture* (1986) and also in *The Unwins Book of Sweet Peas* by Colin Hambidge (1996). I regret to say that both are wrong but must also admit that I too was wrong when I put the same notion into print more recently myself. Charles Unwin reported "wild" sweet peas in Malta but there seems little doubt that these were the result of escape from gardens. They are not even comfortably naturalized there as it seems they are unusually difficult to grow in Malta owing to a soil-borne disease.

Other locations suggested for the origin of sweet peas have been China, as recently as 1985, and also South America: the variety 'Quito' was collected from a garden in that city, the capital of Ecuador; 'Matucana' was found in a place of that name in Peru. Confusingly, in an echo of the naming of *Scilla peruviana*, which originates in Spain, Portugal and Morocco, 'Sicilian Pink' and 'Sicilian Fuchsia' were also found at Matucana in Peru – they were named in honour of Francisco Cupani. These were undoubtedly the descendants of introductions by early colonists.

The original colour of these plants is described by Commelin, from plants he raised from Cupani's seed, as having 'a purple standard, the remaining petals are sky blue'. Ray describes them as 'with a red standard; the lip-like petals surrounding the keel are pale blue'. Early illustrations confirm this although, of course, the colour cannot be firmly established from early herbarium specimens. It has been inferred from some texts that there was also a white form; the non-existent form from Sri Lanka was said to be a pink and white bicolour.

In the 1970s the sweet pea pioneer Dr Keith Hammett collected seed of wild sweet peas from Sicily and these are now available under the name 'Original' or 'Cupani's Original'. If you want to grow the true wild sweet pea, this is it.

Early developments in gardens

The first sweet peas were offered for sale in 1724 as 'sweet sented pease', and the first cultivar name, 'Painted Lady', is found in the writings of Philip Miller in 1731 who describes it as 'pale red' and who also mentions the white form; so, with Cupani's original, that makes three distinct forms in cultivation at this time. In 1775 a scarlet one is mentioned, in 1778 a seedsman offered the same white, purple and 'Painted Lady', while in 1782 another seedsman is recorded as selling all four: scarlet, white, purple and 'Painted Lady'.

It seems extraordinary but by 1788 William Curtis was writing in the *Botanical Magazine*: "There is scarcely a plant more generally cultivated than the Sweet Pea... general cultivation extends to

two only, one with blossoms perfectly white, and the other white and rose-coloured, commonly called the 'Painted Lady Pea'."

In 1793 John Mason, founder of the company which eventually evolved into the Hurst breeders and packet seed brand, and who traded from a pub in London's Fleet Street (how the seed trade has changed...), listed five varieties: purple, white, 'Painted Lady', scarlet and black; the "black" was probably a dark purple or maroon. By the time of Philip Miller's *The Gardener's Dictionary* in 1807 there is an interesting mention of the height of the sweet peas of that time – which is given as "from three to four feet high". Modern varieties are noticeably taller, even when poorly grown, so it is clear that over the years breeders and gardeners have tended to select the more vigorous plants from which to save seed, so increasing the height of plants. This point also tends to support the view that the 'Painted Lady' we grow today, which is as tall as other varieties, is not a direct descendant of the original form, but a later throwback from a more modern variety. This is reinforced by the fact that Miller also quotes them all as having just two flowers per stem (as has Dr Hammett's recent introduction from Sicily); in many cases breeders have increased this to three or four.

The year of 1840 seems to mark the end of the first phase of development, most of which took place more or less by chance. At this time *The Ladies' Flower Garden of Ornamental Annuals* gives the following account: "There are six distinct kinds of sweet peas in constant cultivation, all of which, with very few exceptions, come true from seed. There are the purple, which has a standard of deep reddish purple, the wings pinkish, and the keel nearlywhite...; the New Painted Lady, which has a standard of a deep rose colour, the wings pale rose, and the keel pure white...; the Old Painted Lady, which has wings and keel white and the standard flesh-coloured; the blue, which has the wings and keel a pale blue and the standard dark bluish purple; and the violet, which has the keel pale violet, the wings a deep violet, and the standard a dark reddish purple."

In 1837 James Carter of Holborn in London, the founder of what became Carters Tested Seeds, introduced the first flaked variety (then called striped) and by 1860 he listed nine varieties plus the first "yellow", in fact cream, and another said to be the result of crossing *L. odoratus* with the blue-flowered perennial *L. nervosus* (Lord Anson's pea), from South America. Such a cross has never been made but the "result" was named 'Blue Edged'. Re-christened 'Blue Hybrid', this wired variety with a slender margin of blue on an otherwise white flower was awarded a First Class Certificate (the top award) by the Royal Horticultural Society in 1883.

It was not the first sweet pea to gain an RHS award. 'Scarlet Invincible', in fact more carmine than scarlet, gained an FCC in 1867; at this time development was starting to hasten. In 1870 James Vick of Rochester, New York, listed scarlet, scarlet striped with white, white, purple striped with white, 'Painted Lady', 'Blue Edged', black, black with light blue, and 'Scarlet Invincible'. In 1878 Suttons introduced 'Butterfly', similar to 'Blue Edged', and in all by 1881, as things began to gather pace, there were 21: purple, white, large dark purple, scarlet, black, purple striped white, 'New Painted Lady', 'Large Dark Purple', yellow, 'Blue Edged', 'Scarlet Invincible', scarlet striped with white, 'Black Invincible', 'Crown Princess of Russia', 'Fairy Queen', 'Purple Invincible', 'Invincible Striped Violet Queen', 'Heterosperma', 'The Queen', 'Captain Clarke', and 'Imperial Purple'.

These varieties had either plain upright standards or hooded standards, some with symmetrical notches towards their base; the wings tended to be folded around the keel.

Henry Eckford and the coming of the Grandifloras

As the century approached its turn, an ever-increasing number of varieties appeared. Some were only listed for a year or two before disappearing, some were named and never listed by commercial seed houses but distributed personally, soon to fade away. It seems clear that, as is so often the case when a new flower captures the public's attention (and its purses), many "new" introductions were no better, and little different from their predecessors.

'Invincible Carmine' from Thomas Laxton of Bedford (better known for his 'Laxton's Superb' and other apples) was a significant introduction which was awarded an FCC in 1883, and is also notable as the first variety to be the result of deliberate hand pollination. And 1882 saw the award of an FCC to the first of Henry Eckford's introductions, 'Bronze Prince'.

Eckford transformed the flower, developing improved form, larger size and new colours yet retaining the fragrance which was such a striking feature of the original wild species. By 1900 he had introduced 115 varieties out of a total grown at the time, including many highly transient varieties, of 264. Henry Eckford had success with breeding other flowers before his involvement with the sweet pea; while head gardener to the Earl of Radnor, he raised many new varieties of pelargonium, verbena and dahlia. He then went to work for Dr Sankey of Sandywell near Gloucester specifically to raise new varieties. He arrived in 1870 and set methodically to crossing, selecting and fixing new varieties; 'Bronze Prince' was the first to be released. He

'Prima Donna', a classic Grandiflora and at the end of the 19th century considered one of the best.

CHOICE
SWEET
PEAS

D.W. Croll
DUNDEE, SCOTLAND

A. Model
B. Sunkist
C. Pinkie
D. Powerscourt
E. Picture
F. Mrs. A. Searles
G. Reflection
H. Grenadier
I. Sybil Henshaw
J. Olympia

THE
GLORIA
COLLECTION

This page from the catalogue of D.W. Croll of Aberdeen shows part of the range of sweet peas available in 1936.

moved with the doctor to Shropshire, then in 1888 set up his breeding and trials fields in the Shropshire town of Wem.

In the years until the end of the century Eckford raised a generous succession of Grandiflora sweet peas, so called because their flowers were noticeably larger than those few derived directly from Cupani's original. These included 'Princess of Wales' (1888), 'Captain of the Blues' (1889), 'Prima Donna' (1896) and 'Lady Grisel Hamilton' (1898).

The powerful demand from the United States for new varieties soon began to drive Eckford's work. In 1886 his varieties were offered in the United States by James Breck and in the early 1890s demand took off, led by the enthusiasm of the Reverend W. T. Hutchins. He, Breck, Peter Henderson, W. Atlee Burpee, D. M. Ferry, the Sunset Seed Company, J. C. Vaughan and C. C. Morse & Co, to mention just some of the American seedsmen who took up sweet peas, introduced many of Eckford's varieties and soon began launching their own. In 1897 development in

the United States was also well under way, both W. Atlee Burpee from California and Henry Eckford from Shropshire listing seven new introductions.

Notable American varieties of these times were 'Blanche Ferry' (1889), 'America' (1897), 'Janet Scott' (1903) and 'Flora Norton' (1904); it is clear, even from this short list, that many varieties regarded today as classic old-fashioned English sweet peas, and sometimes even attributed to Eckford, are, in fact, American in origin. It was in this period that Burpee launched the first dwarf variety, 'Cupid' (1893, discovered by Morse, page 27), which was awarded an AM by the RHS.

'Blanche Ferry', developed from 'Old Painted Lady', was actually the first sweet pea to originate in the United States. For 25 years a quarryman's wife in New York State grew 'Painted Lady'; she grew it, and each year she saved her own seed from plants grown, it seems, on limestone ledges where the soil was unusually shallow. After about 15 years the plants developed such compact growth that they no longer needed staking and also tended to produce all their flowers at about the same time. Her selection came to the notice of D. M. Ferry & Co, who introduced the variety as 'Blanche Ferry' in 1889. It was the first sweet pea to be illustrated in colour in an American seed catalogue.

This variety went on to become the progenitor of many American-bred introductions including the early-flowering sorts. In the year that 'Blanche Ferry' was released, a few early-flowering plants were noticed among it on the Ferry trial fields. In 1894 this was introduced as 'Extra Early Blanche Ferry'. Although weak in growth out of doors, under glass it performed well and gave a crop in midwinter.

Development continued and in 1898 W. Atlee Burpee introduced 'Earliest of All', also derived from 'Blanche Ferry', followed in 1902 by 'Extreme Early, Earliest of All'. By this time the tendency of seedsmen to hyperbolize was all too evident. These were the precursors of the winter-flowering kinds and Anton C. Zvolaneck, originally in New Jersey and later in California, was instrumental in creating these, at first by crossing an early-flowering selection of 'Lottie Eckford' with 'Blanche Ferry'. All these 'earlies' were of Grandiflora type until, in 1913, Anton Zvolaneck released his early-flowering Spencers; 'Zvolaneck's Rose' was the outstanding early variety of the era. Frank Cuthbertson worked on the same group for C. C. Morse & Co, as did Dr J. H. Franklin for Waller-Franklin and George Kerr for W. Atlee Burpee.

Soon after the release of 'Blanche Ferry', in 1896 James Vicks' Sons introduced the first "double"-flowered variety, the effect created by the presence of an extra standard, sometimes two, and today referred to as duplex; this too was derived from 'Blanche Ferry'; it was named 'Bride of Niagara' although W. T. Hutchins in a contemporary account says, with a tone of slight condescension: "It does produce about 30 per cent of so-called doubles." He continued: "Many of the improved varieties, when well grown, show a vigour of habit that sometimes makes double stems, but oftener they break up the standard of the blossom into several imperfect standards, and occasionally the wings are duplicated. No sound dictum of taste would consider this an advantage or an improvement in this flower."

Development continued apace, and in 1911 an astonishing total of 135 new introductions were made in the United States and Britain combined.

The Spencer sweet pea

By 1900 sweet peas were sufficiently popular in Britain for a Sweet Pea Bi-Centenary Celebration to be staged in London. This must have been a staggering event. One of the competitive classes called for 100 bunches of sweet peas in ten different shades; another for 48 bunches in no fewer than 36 varieties. There was even a small subsection for amateurs who actually grew their own flowers rather than employing a gardener! Classes were sponsored by names still known for their sweet peas today: Carters, Suttons and Robert Bolton.

Following this meeting the National Sweet Pea Society (NSPS) was formed, and the following year, in 1901, held its first show – at the Royal Aquarium in Westminster! The hall is now known as the Central Hall, Westminster.

The day before the show opened rumours began to spread around the hall about a revolutionary new sweet pea. Silas Cole did little but tease the other exhibitors and it was not until a few

minutes before the deadline the following morning that he staged his table decoration of his new variety – which stunned everyone.

His 'Countess Spencer' was deep rose pink in colour and a contemporary report stated that "it seemed as if nature has been so lavish that the material in its standard had to be closely pleated to hold it in position. It was beflowered and befrilled." So the waved standard had arrived and although Eckford's Grandifloras, and those from other breeders, continued to dominate in number for some years, in impact 'Countess Spencer' and its derivatives were instantly the favourites.

Silas Cole was Head Gardener for the Earl Spencer at Althorp Park in Northamptonshire, as had been his father before him. A leading exhibitor of flowers, in 1898 he crossed two popular Grandifloras of the time, 'Lovely' and 'Triumph', and saved the seed. In the following year he picked out a few promising seedlings, and these he crossed with Eckford's 'Prima Donna'. He sowed the seeds, and in 1900 when he inspected his rows of one of the

'Superfine' (left) and 'Smiles', two novelties from Unwins Seeds for the autumn of 1933.

resulting seedlings, he found one plant that was more vigorous, and later flowering, than the others. Cole was astonished to see that the flowers were much larger than his Grandifloras, by about 25 per cent, and that the standards were noticeably ruffled. Of course, he saved seed – just one pod, containing five seeds.

The following year he sowed his five seeds: three were eaten by mice, but from the resulting two plants he cut enough blooms of what he named 'Countess Spencer' to take to the first NSPS show at the Royal Aquarium. It was unanimously awarded an FCC.

He saved 90 seeds that year, sowed them in 1902 and, astonishingly, every one is said to have come true. But it was a cold, wet summer and his 90 plants produced only 3,000 seeds. Two thousand two hundred of these were sold to Robert Sydenham of Birmingham who sent them to America to be bulked up in a more suitable climate. They came back startlingly mixed.

Silas Cole himself, writing in NSPS *Annual* for 1906, while mentioning that 'no variety introduced in recent years was received with such a chorus of approval' also admits that 'no variety has caused more disappointment and annoyance' owing to its habit of sporting. He attempts to promote this as a 'blessing in disguise' but to most it was indeed a disappointment.

The year after Silas Cole found his sport, W. J. Unwin, a cut-flower grower at Histon near Cambridge in England, returned home from church one Sunday morning and took a stroll through the rows of sweet peas growing alongside his house on what was then called Dog Kennel Lane, now the Impington Road. There he spotted a similar, but not identical, variant in his rows of 'Prima Donna' grown for cut flowers. The flower he noticed was pale pink, slightly larger than the flowers of 'Prima Donna', and with its petals slightly waved. His son Charles W. J. Unwin specifically makes the point in the early editions of his book that this was a sport and not the result of hybridization.

W. J. Unwin used this breakthrough as the foundation for a business selling sweet pea seed, rather than cut flowers. He named his find 'Gladys Unwin', after his elder daughter, and, after ensuring that it was properly fixed and true, it was introduced.

The Unwins Type of sweet pea was popular for some years and, between 1905 and 1909, 15 varieties were introduced, most, but not all, raised by W. J. Unwin. But the larger form and extra waviness of the Spencer type dominated and W. J. Unwin himself developed Spencers, incorporating blood from the Unwins type, to create an increasing range of, fixed, Spencer varieties.

So two similar waved forms were found in 1900 and 1901, both associated with 'Prima Donna'. But what, you might ask, was Henry Eckford doing while all this was going on at Althorp and Histon? Becoming nervous of his place as the pre-eminent sweet pea breeder in the world, perhaps. For a Mr E. Viner, an amateur gardener from Frome in Somerset, also found a waved type. It is worth quoting from a letter from Mr Viner to William Cuthbertson, of Dobbie & Co in Edinburgh:

"It must have been the spring of 1900.
I procured a few seeds of Prima Donna and
Lovely, with the object of choosing the one
I liked the best, and my choice fell on Prima
Donna. I quite discarded Lovely.
The following year I grew Prima Donna
from seed I saved myself, and quite late in
the season I noticed a spray of two blooms on
Prima Donna at the extremity of a shoot with a
peculiarly crimpled character.
I marked them and allowed it to seed
(no other flowers appeared), and I obtained
seven good seeds. The following year I planted
them in due course and all germinated, and to
my delight five retained the wavy character; the
other two were Prima Donna pure.
But the waved ones were glorious in the fine
weather of early July... at the suggestion of
others it was named Nellie Viner. Later in the
season I sent blooms to Mr Eckford, to whom
I eventually sold. Therefore, Mr Eckford's variety
was a sport from Prima Donna."

In recognition of his important contribution to the development of the sweet pea, when Mr Viner became ill about ten years later and no longer able to earn his living, a testimonial collection was organized by a committee of the NSPS and raised £70.

So Henry Eckford's form, the third of this ruffled trio, said to be a hooded form and one of the largest flowered of its type, and one which consistently produced four flowers per stem, he bought from Mr Viner – and then sold it not as 'Nellie Viner' but as 'Countess Spencer'. Strangely, 'Nellie Viner' is still grown today but seems more like an Unwin type, or a very slightly waved Grandiflora, than an early Spencer.

It seems extraordinary that this break should occur in three different places, originating in two different ways (though both involving 'Prima Donna'), and resulting in three different forms at almost exactly the same time. The Unwin type was between the Grandiflora type and 'Countess Spencer' both in size and the degree of waviness of the standards. But there was also one other, perhaps more crucial, difference. Before W. J. Unwin released his variety, he ensured that it was fixed and uniform. So by contrast with 'Countess Spencer', growers could be sure of the result of sowing seed of 'Gladys Unwin' rather than be faced with the unpredictability of 'Countess Spencer'. It was this dependability which was the foundation for the creation, in 1903, of the company which became the Unwins Seeds of today, still the leading retailer of sweet peas and trading from the same site on which his 'Prima Donna' sweet peas were grown.

After the revolution

There followed a great burst of enthusiasm for sweet peas, especially the Spencer type. For some years both the Grandifloras and the Spencer types continued to be developed; new Spencers arose through back-crossing 'Countess Spencer' on to Grandifloras of various colours to increase the colour range of Spencers and then by making crosses between Spencers, and also isolating sports.

In 1911 Lord Northcliffe, owner of the *Daily Mail*, offered a prize of £1,000 for the finest bunch of 12 spikes of sweet peas; entries were restricted to amateurs who employed not more than a single gardener. At the competition at the Crystal Palace in London, 35,000 entries were received. An expert committee of ten sweet pea growers narrowed the

entries first to 10,000 and selected 1,003 for awards. The first prize went to Mrs Denholm Fraser of Kelso in Scotland; her husband, the Reverend D. Denholm Fraser, won third prize with blooms from the same garden – and it was he, not his wife, who published a small book capitalizing on his success.

The new Spencer types soon dominated although Grandifloras continued to be raised as the enthusiasm for sweet peas continued. Between 1921 and 1925, over 600 stocks of sweet peas were trialled at the RHS garden at Wisley. With, understandably, insufficient space to grow them all in one season the stocks were divided into colour groups and a different range grown each year. This number included almost no Cupids and no early flowering sorts. Later, in 1931, a staggering 321 stocks were grown for trial. At this time, to avoid the confusion occasioned by the constant influx of new introductions, the NSPS issued an annual List of Too-much Alike Varieties; such a list would still be useful today.

In the United States, new types were developed: some were more tolerant of the hot summers that both the Spencers and Grandifloras found uncomfortable, others were developed for cropping as cut flowers under glass.

Since the Spencers took over, breeders around the world have introduced varieties with larger flowers, flowers in a better and more consistent form, flowers with greater substance to the petals, flowers better placed on the stem for exhibition, and more consistent in producing four flowers per stem even in less than careful culture. Vigour has been improved and contemporary varieties grow to almost twice the height of early, pre-Spencer sweet peas in even average cultural conditions. Colours too have improved, from the purest white through every shade of pink to orange and red, plus many shades of lavender and blue through to almost black, these colours combining with the other attributes to constantly improve the flower.

There is still a continuous stream of new introductions from both amateur and professional breeders. One of the factors driving the introduction of new varieties is that each of the major retail seed companies, and the sweet pea specialists, likes to have its own unique varieties; inevitably this leads to what non-specialists at least view as duplication.

Since the arrival of the Spencers, other classes of sweet peas that have emerged include the early-flowering varieties such as the Cuthbertsons (page 35), important in many regions of the United States as they flower before the summer heat becomes too intense; productive cut-flower types like the Royals (page 37), the tendril-free types like Snoopea (page 88), Supersnoop (page 89) and Explorer (page 59) and the more recent New Century Series (page 75); a range of Intermediate types reaching about 90cm/3ft height, in particular the Jet Set Series (page 66); Multiflora types with up to 11, but more often six to eight, flowers on a stem like the Early Multiflora Giganteas (page 35) and Galaxys (page 35). And now there is a resurgence of interest in dwarf types derived from Cupids, originally introduced in 1898 (page 27).

Classic larger-flowered waved varieties that followed the original 'Countess Spencer' and 'Gladys Unwin' include 'Mrs C. Kay', 'Noel Sutton', 'Nora Holman', 'Mrs R. Bolton', 'Mrs Bernard Jones', 'Jilly', 'Midnight', 'Windsor', 'Leamington', 'Southampton' and more. And after many years in which the Grandifloras were largely neglected, since the 1980s interest in this group has revived and the original varieties, or replicas of them, have been reintroduced. Now a number of breeders including Peter Grayson, Unwins and E. W. King are again introducing new varieties in the Grandiflora style.

In modern times

The development of sweet peas in modern times can be conveniently split into three strands. In Britain, breeding has been almost exclusively in the Spencer sweet peas, with some interest in dwarfer types and a recent revival in Grandifloras; in the United States there has been a greater interest in semi-dwarf or intermediate types and on tall types for commercial production and varieties which tolerate the summer heat. In New Zealand, thanks to one man, Dr Keith Hammett, bicolours, 'fancy' kinds and the search for a yellow sweet pea have predominated.

In Britain the development of Spencer types has been driven partly by tradition, partly by the conservative nature of the British gardening public and partly by exhibitors who, until recently, have tended to drive the awards process. This has resulted in the virtues of long strong stems, limited number of flowers on the stem, placement of flowers on the stem, the form of flowers, and response to cordon culture taking precedence over qualities such as long flowering season, many flowers on a stem, tolerance of failure to dead-head, long vase-life and long stems for cutting on semi-dwarf plants.

In recent years two other groups have been developed in Britain: Grandifloras and dwarf types. Peter Grayson has rescued, popularized and made available many old original Grandifloras and has also raised new varieties in the old style. Unwins Seeds and E. W. King have also raised new Grandifloras and some of these are very effective garden plants.

At the same time, E. W. King was a pioneer of the semi-dwarf, tendril-free type with Snoopea and has recently revived this group with their New Century Constellation Series. 'Pink Cupid' has also been revived and has proved popular as a garden centre plant, seedlings being sold in striking pink pots. Tony Hender of British plant breeders Floranova and then Seedlynx has gone on to develop a modern series of Cupid types. Amateur breeder Andrew Beane is also working on this group, with particular emphasis on striped dwarfs, as seen in his Pinocchio Series. Dwarf types are also coming into Western Europe from Russia, winning awards and being made available in the West.

Tall tendril-free types have recently made a reappearance. Harvey Albutt's 'Astronaut' won an AM at Wisley in 1989, then Thompson & Morgan developed his work into a consistent range of colours released as a mixture, 'Astronaut Mixed', in 2002. It remains to be seen if the flowers are of sufficiently high quality to please exhibitors, for it is exhibitors who routinely remove tendrils and so would perhaps appreciate naturally tendril-free plants. Oddly, Peter Grayson introduced a pale blue, tall, tendril-free type called 'Spaceman' in 1997.

In the United States, the emphasis has been

different. The necessity to develop varieties which cope with the harsh summer climate of many areas has led to the creation of series like the Cuthbertsons which better tolerate summer heat and Winter Elegance which flower more quickly from seed so can mature in the short period between spring thaw and summer heat.

Here the commercial cut-flower market has also been a driver and the Royal and Bouquet series have been a success both in the USA and around the world. Semi-dwarf (Intermediate) types have also been repeatedly improved; 'Jet Set' was outstanding and for many years was available in separate colours.

'Supersnoop', an improvement on the tendril-free 'Snoopea', has been very successful and followed more recently by the Explorer Series with its impressive colours, impact and longer stems. Although winning many awards for the separate colours at RHS trials, these spectacular varieties are not widely available. Much shorter mixtures like

When stocks are not rogued thoroughly by seed growers, off types occur in the garden; this is supposed to be 'Queen Alexandra', but contains many pink rogues.

Patio, Little Sweetheart and more have occasionally gripped gardeners' attention but largely remain relegated to the few last lines of the catalogue.

Development in New Zealand has been the work of British breeder Dr Keith Hammett. His series of bicolours, followed by his reverse bicolours and flakes, all with the emphasis on fragrance, have been developed in parallel with his work towards a yellow sweet pea using the recently discovered *Lathyrus belinensis* (page 94).

Chapter Two
Fragrance

Every few years, there is another anguished lament about modern sweet peas having no scent; the same cry is regularly heard about roses. This is perhaps more a case of the complainants losing their sense of smell, or gaining an enhanced sense of nostalgia, than the plants losing their fragrance.

People have been making this complaint for many decades. In 1927 Norman Lambert and H. H. Thomas state in their *Sweet Peas for Amateurs*: "So much is written, and so much said unnecessarily, about loss of scent in the modern sweet pea that it is hardly worth the controversy. The modern sweet pea is still *sweet*." Charles W. J. Unwin, in the 1929 edition of *Sweet Peas: Their History, Development, Culture*, seems to suggest that it would be a bad thing if they were more strongly scented: "To my mind, an increase of actual strength of scent would be a detriment and not a gain." By the time of the publication of the 1986 edition of that same book, Charles Unwin seems to have changed his mind: "There is the somewhat alarming fact that the coming of the Spencer type brought with it a certain loss of perfume... I feel sure that there has been a gradual loss of scent ever since." Then, as recently as 1996, in *The Unwins Book of Sweet Peas*, Colin Hambidge says: "Sweet peas with a strong scent are still being bred and introduced to gardeners."

I agree with Colin Hambidge. It is simply not true that modern varieties of sweet peas have lost their perfume. What is true is that varieties vary in their strength of fragrance: some are faint, others well scented, others intensely fragrant. In the 1990s a wide range of strongly scented Spencers has been introduced, 'Gwendoline' and 'Edward Unwin' to name but two, along with new Grandifloras and even dwarfs with a strong scent. And research at the Department of Biological Sciences at Stirling University has concluded that there has been no loss of fragrance in modern varieties – a conclusion based on comparing the original wild sweet pea with a number of modern Spencers, but especially with 'Old Times'.

It is remarkable that the researchers, who published their results in 2001, discovered that no one had ever actually analysed the chemical constituents that make up the fragrance of sweet peas. Naturally, they immediately set out to do just that and discovered six major components together with 12 minor ones. What will perhaps surprise the gardener and the interested "sniffer" is that there seems to be no single component which makes sweet peas smell the way they do. The six major components are all known to be part of the make-up of the perfume of other plants: ocimene is found in basil, hops and tagetes; linalool is found in lavender, daphne and jasmine; phenyacetaldehyde is found in oil seed rape and honey; geraniol is found in roses and geraniums; nerol is found in orange and magnolia; citronellol is found in damask roses.

It is the balance of these major ingredients, together with the minor ones, which gives sweet peas their unique fragrance. The research also looked at the fragrance of a relatively unscented variety, 'Diana', and found that even a weight of flowers twice that of the wild sweet pea tested produced only seven fragrance ingredients out of a possible 18. No wonder the smell in 'Diana' is almost non-existent.

Clearly sweet pea fragrance depends not only upon the presence of certain chemicals but also on their quantity and balance. There is no doubt that the factors which create scent are still found in modern varieties, and so if varieties are introduced that are relatively unscented this is entirely the choice of the breeder – who clearly feels that other features of the variety compensate for this shortfall. It is also worth saying that there has hardly been a sweet pea introduced that has absolutely no scent at all; it may be faint but it will be there.

Sweet pea fragrance is best appreciated on a dry, sunny day. Cool weather and a damp atmosphere tend to reduce fragrance and when the flowers are cut, fragrance is often diminished, so it would be unwise to judge the perfume of a variety from two-day-old stems in a vase indoors.

Many catalogues now grade their varieties and, although each uses a different system, the only necessity is perhaps to view with a little caution the occasional hyperbolic overenthusiasm; the aim, after all, is to sell seed.

It is true, however, that scent tends to be associated with some types more than others. In particular Grandifloras tend to be strongly scented while dwarfs tend to be poorly scented. This, I have to stress, is a very general rule and there are many varieties which do not fit.

List of especially well-scented varieties

The list of descriptions (page 38) rates a good range of varieties as 'strongly scented'; in addition the following lists may be helpful.

Of the Spencer types, I especially recommend: 'Edward Unwin', 'Enid Walker', 'Evensong', 'Fragrantissima', 'Gwendoline', 'Honeymoon', 'Memorial Flight', 'Old Times', 'Pamela', 'Richard and Judy'.

The American writer Tovah Martin, a specialist on old-fashioned flowers, has trialled many sweet peas in her own garden in Connecticut and recommends: 'Black Knight', 'Blanche Ferry', 'Cupani Original', 'Flora Norton', 'Old Spice Mixed', 'Painted Lady', 'Royal Family'.

Sunset magazine, based in California, recommends the following for fragrance:
Grandifloras: 'Black Knight', 'Butterfly', 'Cupani', 'Cupani's Original', 'Dorothy Eckford', 'Lady Grisel Hamilton', 'Painted Lady', 'Perfume Delight'.
Spencers: 'Angela Ann', 'Annabelle', 'Frolic', 'Jilly', 'King Size Navy', 'Mollie Rilstone', 'Nora Holman', 'Percy Thrower', 'White Supreme'.

'Aurora', a flaked variety popular in the United States in the late 19th century.

Chapter Three
In the garden

The sweet pea is an adaptable flower. The tall varieties are vigorous and resilient, the intermediates are determinedly bushy, the dwarfs neat but tough. If the aim is to create an attractive garden feature, rather than grow them for exhibition, and to integrate them into the garden scene, there are many ways of going about it.

Cordons for cut flowers and exhibition

It is undeniable that the best-quality flowers, on the longest stems, are grown by the cordon method (page 108), which is the method of choice for exhibitors. But is a row of sweet peas grown on canes an attractive garden feature or an eyesore?

In the early stages, it's true, a row of cordon sweet peas is no more than a row of canes and this may seem an ugly feature. But if the canes are neatly and evenly set in place, and most particularly if they are arranged vertically (page 109), a row of cordons can make an inoffensive feature even from the day the structure is completed. Use rustic poles instead and many will consider the structure attractive.

As the plants grow and come into flower, clearly the appearance improves. But with the removal of tendrils and sideshoots, necessary to encourage exhibition-quality flowers, there will never be a mass of green foliage to please the onlooker. The flowers will all tend to be carried at the same height, so the colour will fall in a band across the plot, and with cutting or dead-heading practised necessarily ruthlessly, there will be no effervescence of colour.

A delightful planting of sweet peas trained on a steel archway at Helmingham Hall, Suffolk.

However, as a divider across a vegetable garden, at the back of an annual border (inasmuch as gardeners grow such a thing any more – in spite of decades of my urging), or even along a pathway where maintenance is easily accomplished, a row of cordons can look attractive as long as the structure is built with care and symmetry. The trick, from the point of view of integrating a row of cordons into the garden, is to allow a space for access along the row and then plant a row of plants (Intermediate sweet peas, even) which, as they develop, will hide the bare stems at the base of the cordons.

Grown freely on wire

Purists are against growing sweet peas on galvanized wire netting; they say that in the heat of the summer the wire becomes so hot that it damages stems and flowers. This can be true. But really... so the occasional stem or flower is singed. Is that so very crucial? This method is so productive that the loss of the occasional stem can surely be overlooked – if it's noticed at all.

And not only productive. This is by far the most attractive method of growing sweet peas in large quantities and although the flower quality and stem length may be less impressive than on plants grown on cordons, the more modest expertise required has a great deal to recommend them.

The wire must be set up securely, with stout posts, the ground prepared well in advance and, if possible, a length of seephose laid along the row to facilitate effective and efficient watering. If plastic netting is substituted, the posts must be closer together to support this relatively limp material.

The result will be a billowing mass of colour. While this approach can be used to create a divider in the vegetable garden, it looks especially spectacular where a screen is required along pathways. It also makes a more impressive background to an annual, or perennial, border and it is relatively simple to construct the support on a curve, on a wave, or for it to turn a corner and strike off in a new direction. Using it as a background to a corner-sited annual border can be sensational.

'Queen Alexandra' growing on netting erected in front of a hornbeam hedge at the Royal Horticultural Society's gardens at Wisley, Surrey.

Ideally, a planting is made either for the garden or for the house. Cutting a few stems for the house hardly diminishes the garden effect, but the temptation is always to fill the house with flowers.

When the need is for cut flowers, and the row is sited in isolation from other flowers, choosing the appropriate varieties is mainly a matter of selecting favourites and arranging them so that their colours, and those of other neighbouring plants, associate well together. This is one of the few situations in which mixtures are appropriate, although the impact on the viewer can be confused by the sheer range of different colours jostling for attention.

If mixtures are your preferred route, there are a number of options. You can pick a mixture that contains just about every colour and form: I found 'Horizon' to be especially varied in colour with selfs, bicolours, stripes and flakes all in a good range of shades *and* with scent. 'Flower Arrangers' Blend', and others with similar names, also include a wide range.

There are also colour-themed mixtures such as 'Rhapsody in Blue', 'Pink Reflections', 'Sunset Blend' and 'Rosemary Verey' if flowers in a narrower range of shades are preferred. Or try the 'Full Stop' mixture, featuring stripes combined with self colours in matching shades.

When the aim is also for an attractive garden display, then the colours of the different varieties must not only look good alongside each other but must also associate well with the annuals or perennials for which they provide a background. And if clumps of tall foreground plants are placed so that they straddle the area where two different varieties of sweet peas sit alongside each other on the wire, then a vibrant and attractive display will be the result.

It matters not whether Grandifloras, originals or modern introductions, or Spencers are chosen. The ruffled flower form of the Spencers will hardly be visible at the back of a border, although the sheer size of the flowers of many varieties is an important consideration. The productivity of the

Grandifloras, and of those sometimes known as Multifloras, might be thought more valuable, though towards the end of the season their naturally slightly smaller flowers will become smaller still as the plants tend to run out of energy.

So, for example, *Lavatera* 'Silver Cup' looks superb in front of the white Multiflora 'Jimmy Young' (it must be a pure white, since 'Silver Cup' makes creams look muddy), with the soft blue 'Cambridge Blue' alongside. The tall and slender annual white lupin 'Biancaneve' can go alongside the lavatera (the contrast in habit is in itself striking) and in front of the blue sweet pea, with perhaps one of the old original Grandifloras like 'Prima Donna' next along the row.

It is important, when growing sweet peas in this way, to prepare and to look after them well. They can make an enormous amount of growth and produce a vast quantity of flowers, so a decent trench with plenty of organic matter is helpful, as is regular watering, and regular picking or dead-heading.

However, having said all that, it is also essential to emphasize that even with minimal preparation, irregular watering and little or no feeding, it is still possible to create a colourful and fragrant show of sweet peas. For too long, gardeners have been put off by believing it necessary to take extravagant pains when growing sweet peas. This is not so.

Wigwams for cut flowers

I am always slightly mystified as to the popularity of wigwams (page 106), although the easy availability of the materials and the lack of skill required in construction is definitely appealing. When planted for cutting, in many ways wigwams make more practical features in the vegetable garden as they cast so much less shade than long stretches of canes or wire.

Individual varieties can be chosen for each structure, but it is often more practical to choose two that look good together: select the varieties you like to cut, then pair them off to their best advantage.

One of the earliest Grandifloras, 'Violet Queen', trained through birch brushwood in a mixed planting at Wisley.

If there is space for just one, it can be tempting to choose one of the mixtures suggested earlier. But mixtures work best when a relatively large number of plants are grown, so maximizing the chance of finding that all the elements of the blend are present when the plants come into flower.

When a limited number of plants are grown, as on a single wigwam, it pays to select the varieties more carefully, perhaps just three or four, or even only two, to be sure of growing a range which fits your needs. You will often find that collections of varieties, packed separately, are an economical way of providing a range of flowers for cutting in a small space.

Wigwams in borders

Wigwams make poor features in a border. This is not to say that structures supporting just one variety do not make an impact, since they can be spectacular in terms of both colour and scent, but the wigwam is not the structure to achieve this (page 107). An arrangement in which the canes, or other supports, are set vertically gives the plants more space to show themselves off to the best advantage or, better still, a wire tower reduces the visual dominance of the structure itself relative to the flowers – and, after all, it's the flowers that are important. A single variety on each structure is surely the best option; mixtures look messy and it's impossible to relate them harmoniously to the plantings around them.

In the border, these features fill the role of a very tall annual or perennial or shrub. They will tend to be sited towards the middle or rear of the border, although as a feature on a front corner or by a gateway they can be invaluable; but the choice of type and variety needs to be related to the situation.

For a wigwam or tower feature in the middle or at the back of a border, self colours, or clearly defined bicolours, are the most effective; the detailed patterning in the stripes and flakes is not usually visible at a distance and so their special features remain unappreciated. I would also be wary of gentle picotees, which are often wasted viewed from afar. If scent is an important feature, select varieties with the very strongest fragrance, which will reach the path from the back of the border.

An alternative way of growing sweet peas freely on columns, a ring of pig netting is supported by three stout bamboo canes.

My own choice for this situation would be varieties like 'Mrs Bernard Jones' (bright pink), 'Royal Wedding' (white), 'Charlie's Angel' (soft blue), 'Midnight' (deep maroon) and 'Robert Uvedale' (carmine).

Towards the front of the border, by gateways, or for forward focal points, varieties with a more detailed patterning which can be appreciated at close quarters, and with scent, come into their own. Well-scented stripes like 'Aquarius' (lavender blue) and 'Pulsar' (rich carmine mauve), 'Champagne Bubbles' (creamy amber), also well scented, and 'Romeo' (white, edged purple) with its spectacular scent, all qualify here.

On fences and walls

It always surprises me that sweet peas are not grown more frequently on walls and fences. True, these situations pose problems of their own, but in small town and suburban gardens this is surely the way to grow both the classic Spencers and the Grandiflora sweet peas. Sufficient light and rain must be available to ensure success, but too much sun and heat will encourage mildew.

Two kinds of shade prevail in smaller gardens. Sweet peas are unhappy under the shade of overhanging trees and will not thrive there. However, on fences and walls which benefit from little or no direct sun but which are nevertheless open to the sky and not shaded by walls or shrubs to the side, sweet peas can thrive.

Walls and fences often cast a 'rain shadow' so that plants whose roots are close to the base are deprived of natural moisture. Couple this with the tendency of borders in small gardens to be especially crowded with plants, whose roots all compete for the same moisture, and you can see that the sweet peas may suffer. There are three ways to solve the problem.

The first is to prepare well, incorporating plenty of moisture-retentive organic matter into the soil before planting, and then mulching well afterwards. This will help provide the roots with a reservoir of moisture.

The second approach is set up a watering system to help ensure that the plants have all the moisture they need. This can be as simple as sinking a pair of 12.5cm/5in flower pots into the soil on either side of the planting into which water can easily be poured. A short length of seephose or a few drip nozzles connected to a hosepipe can also simplify the necessary watering.

Finally, if space allows, the plants should be set forward from the wall or fence so that the roots are less likely to be 'shadowed' from the rain. This can be tricky in a narrow border and may necessitate some insistent guidance of the shoots as they develop early in the season, to ensure that they find their way to the supports on the wall.

In small gardens, any varieties are suitable but especially those which are scented. On walls which receive little direct sun, varieties that tend to bleach or scorch in brighter conditions will retain their colour well. This especially includes deep and richly coloured varieties like 'Midnight' (deep maroon), and 'Noel Sutton' and 'Oxford Blue' (both dark blue), also scarlet varieties such as 'Red Arrow', 'Barry Dare' and 'Garden News'.

Dark foliage of Atriplex hortensis 'Rubra' is a good foil for white sweet peas like this 'Cream Southbourne'.

On hot and sunny south-facing walls the light and heat can be too fierce and mildew will be rife, though fences retain less heat than walls and so are less punishing. I have found that other annual species of *Lathyrus* can be more resilient. The more slender growth of *L. clymenum* is more suited to scrambling through shrubs, but the picric yellow *L. chloranthus* and the large-flowered *L. tingitanus* should thrive.

But in equable situations, on east and west walls and fences, and where south-facing walls and fences are partially shaded from the side, and on north-facing aspects which are not overhung by trees, the varieties with subtlety, varieties which repay close inspection, are especially suitable. 'Anniversary' (pink picotee on white), 'Gwendoline' (lilac pink), 'Mollie Rilstone' (deep pink picotee on cream), 'Nimbus' (blue-black stripe), 'Rosy Dawn'

Lathyrus tingitanus scrambles through a planting of 'L.D. Braithwaite' rose which provides solid support.

(bright rose flake) and, among new and old Grandifloras, 'Prima Donna' (soft pink), 'Romeo' (white, wired in purple) and 'Juliet' (cream-tinted pink) are especially suitable.

Training into shrubs and climbers

This is a much-neglected way of growing sweet peas, and other annual *Lathyrus* species, in beds and borders. But think about it – this is often the way annual *Lathyrus* grow in nature so why not encourage them to do the same in gardens? The question is: which varieties look best growing through which shrubs and woody climbers?

There are a number of issues to consider. Colour is, of course, top of the list. Which combination of colours creates the best harmony or the boldest contrast? Should the sweet peas be combined with other flowers or with foliage? Are they best

with large leaves or small? Do some shrubs and climbers make better support than others? These are my suggestions, divided up according to the flower colour of the sweet peas.

WHITE There are two approaches to using white sweet peas. I like contrast, and the very first planting I ever made of this type was to set a pot of 'Royal Wedding' at the foot of a purple-leaved form of the smokebush, *Cotinus coggygria*. To be sure of a variety with consistently deep wine-purple foliage choose *C. coggygria* 'Notcutt's Variety' or 'Royal Purple'. This shrub is also nicely twiggy, so providing plenty of support, but if cut back hard every spring to encourage the most luxuriant foliage, the stems can be a little soft to support a mass of sweet pea stems.

Deep green also makes a good background for pure white, and the large leaves of *Aucuba japonica* are ideal – but please, not the various yellow-spotted forms like 'Crotonifolia'; choose a plain green-leaved variety such as 'Rozannie', which stands out for its bold, deep green foliage and, being self-fertile, dependably produces red fruits in winter. To associate with such large foliage, a prolific Multiflora sweet pea such as 'Jimmy Young' looks good, or even a white Grandiflora like 'Mrs Collier'. A fresh green conifer like *Thuja plicata* 'Smaragd', one of the best hedging conifers, also makes a good host.

White clematis make good partners for a white sweet pea: 'Royal Wedding' will bring scent to *Clematis* 'James Mason' or to *C. viticella* 'Alba Luxurians' and the clematis will provide a mass of stems to which the sweet pea can cling. 'Alba Luxurians' often features a hint of mauve, so a scented sweet pea with matching colouring, 'Dragonfly' perhaps, will maintain the colour theme. For a bold contrast, set 'White Supreme' to ramble up through the bright red *C. viticella* 'Mme Julia Correvon'.

To be really cheeky, set plants of a highly scented white Grandiflora like 'Dorothy Eckford' to scramble up through its totally unscented perennial relation *Lathyrus latifolius* 'Albus' to create an illusion of a scented perennial pea.

CREAM Creams are more tricky. Without the purity of white, they are more difficult to set up in contrast to other colours, and creating harmony with other flowers or foliage depends on careful choice of partners.

Choosing a pure white partner has the effect of making the cream look more cream; so the outstanding 'Castle of Mey' can be set to climb up *Abutilon vitifolium* 'Album' or a relatively unscented white climbing rose like 'Climbing Iceberg' which also provides harmony through the fleeting creaminess of its buds.

'Juliet', in cream with a hint of pink, also stands well against pure white or with the relatively unscented rose 'Climbing Cécille Brünner', whose small flowers require a small-flowered pea as partner.

PINK There are so many pink sweet peas (salmon, rose, coral; rich and pale), that this is going to be the colour that gardeners will most want to associate with other plants. And whether the variety is a self like 'Prima Donna', on cream like 'Blushing Bride', on white like 'Gaiety', or is a picotee like

Mixed sweet peas trained on canes fall forward over Chenopodium 'Magentastern'.

'Anniversary' makes a difference. For example, varieties with cream in them do not look as fresh on silver foliage as selfs or those on white; cream on silver or grey just doesn't seem to work.

'Rosy Frills' looks delightful on silver, but being bold and large-flowered, it needs a large-leaved silver to match the impact, perhaps *Elaeagnus augustifolia* again, or *Buddleja fallowiana* with its long, felted foliage, or *Rosa glauca*, which is not exactly grey; but 'Rosy Frills' on a mature *Rosa glauca* really is stunning.

A pink self like 'Angela Ann' or a two-tone pink Grandiflora like 'Painted Lady' would also be spectacular on a *Eucalyptus gunnii*, cut down each spring to promote vigorous foliage growth. A little discreet support might be required as the eucalyptus shoots are not stout.

Try a pink on cream like 'Alan Titchmarsh' or a cream picotee like 'Mollie Rilstone' on a whitebeam like *Sorbus aria* 'Lutescens', cut hard every year to encourage its foliage which is creamy-white on the top side and silver below.

RED Many red varieties have a tendency to fade in bright sun; growing them into a climber or shrub often provides them with a little welcome dappling, and they can also be situated on the west or east side so they are less exposed to the sun's full force.

And here the purple-leaved smokebush comes up again. While a good dark form like 'Royal Purple' sets up a sharp contrast with white-flowered varieties, red-flowered varieties simply add to the sumptuous effect. The best reds for this are probably 'Barry Dare' or 'Red Arrow', or among Grandifloras try 'Queen Alexandra' or even the bright orange 'Henry Eckford'.

Another approach is to use an intermediate variety like 'Explorer Scarlet' or the recent crimson 'Capricorn'. These will fill the low foreground and clamber a little way into the cotinus, creating a happy transition to the rest of the border.

You may feel that this is all a little too sultry, in which case the old Grandiflora flake 'America' would add glints of white light through the basically white ground on which the red streaks are set.

The purple-leaved hazel, *Corylus maxima* 'Purpurea', is more sombre in colour, with few of the glints found in the growing tips of the smokebush. Its twigs are fine but strong and wiry, so support sweet peas well. Here, the scarlet varieties create a more sparky effect, but those in more cerise or carmine shades work better.

ORANGE This is a tricky colour in sweet peas, but one with which you can have a little fun. A mature specimen of golden privet, *Ligustrum ovalifolium* 'Aureum', would make an excellent support especially if pruned regularly, both to keep it stout, so providing good support, and encouraging the best foliage colour without the distraction of creamy flowers. 'Firecrest', with a scarlet undertone to its orange, or the scented 'Orange Surprise' would suit.

Another approach would be to use very dark shrub foliage as a background, such as the purple elder *Sambucus nigra* 'Guincho Purple'. For this use, prune the elder every spring to promote powerful foliage and to eliminate the pink-tinted flowers. The shoots will still be sturdy enough to support the pea.

CERISE AND CARMINE 'Heartbeat', in reddish cerise, 'Garden News', in scarlet with a touch of cerise, 'Robert Uvedale' in deep carmine and the Grandiflora 'Annie B. Gilroy' all look good twining through the purple-leaved hazel. The other approach, of course, is to use the shrub not as support but as a retiring background. For this, a wire wigwam or tower can be set 60–90cm/2–3ft in front of the shrub to set off the sweet peas on their supports.

For gardeners who prefer something with a little more 'startle-factor', a combination of carmine and yellow should do the job. One of our most popular shrubs, *Elaeagnus pungens* 'Maculata', deep green with a bright yellow splash, is stout enough to provide good support; try the prize exhibition variety 'Restormel', in deep cerise, and also excellent in the garden, 'Annie Good' in carmine or the Grandiflora 'Annie B. Gilroy' in cerise. Avoid any with a cream ground like 'First Lady' as this will sit uneasily with the yellow.

To create even more brilliant contrast, choose a purely yellow-leaved shrub. *Choisya* 'Sundance' might seem like an ideal host but its neat and rounded outline provides relatively little available support

Purple-leaved Brassica 'Redbor' makes a mound of curly foliage in front of orange and pink 'Sunset Blend' sweet peas.

for tendrils. There is also the problem of finding yellow foliage which does not scorch in the full sun that sweet peas require in most temperate areas.

Rubus cockburnianus 'Golden Vale' is a superb plant with prettily cut yellow foliage and white stems in winter. Cut it back to the ground in February and it will grow strongly to about1.8m/6ft; plant 'Annie B. Gilroy' at the base in March or April and it follows the yellow foliage up to almost the same height.

Coming down in scale, in a small space or at the front of the border 'Sweetie Carmine' can be set alongside the bright yellow leaves of *Fuchsia magellanica* 'Aurea' – a great small-garden combination.

MAGENTA Varieties in magenta, like 'Carlotta', 'Dynasty' and 'Jayne Amanda', can be used with yellow in the same bold way as the cerise and carmine varieties. Simply to show them off as themselves without the bright contrast is more difficult as, like maroons, they do not always stand out well from plain green.

Training them up a deep yellow climbing rose without a great deal of scent such as 'Good as Gold' or 'Night Light' looks good, and using *Fremontodendron* 'California Glory' as host to 'Jayne Amanda' on a sunny wall really is startling.

MAROON AND 'BLACK' Now this is a challenge. Maroon varieties, and those so dark that they are referred to as black, do not stand out boldly. So, first of all, try to site them in positions where they can be admired closely; at the back of the border they will disappear into the surrounding foliage and shadow and not be appreciated.

But how, exactly, can they be shown off to the best advantage? Well, there's the 'merge and surprise' approach. If you have a purple berberis, *B.* x *ottowensis* 'Superba', perhaps, or the more familiar *B. thunbergii* f. *atropurpurea*, maybe planted on a corner to deter the postman from taking a short cut across the border with his bike on the way to the front door, a scented maroon pea like 'Beaujolais' will partially blend with the foliage in terms of colour but first the scent and then the colour and shape will allow it to stand out.

The other colour which works well with maroon, and which sets up more of a contrast, albeit a soft one, is silver. Silver-leaved shrubs of a suitable size which you might consider planting sufficiently close to a path to see the sweet pea are, however, few and far between. You might use the weeping silver pear, *Pyrus salicifolia* 'Pendula'. This is often planted towards the end of an island bed, or on a corner, as a focal point and 'Beaujolais', or the slightly less scented 'Midnight', would make a great companion.

There are two little tricks you should know when training sweet peas or other annual climbers into weeping shrubs or trees – the same ideas hold when training rambling roses into trees. Firstly, the tips of weeping branches tend to move a great deal, and in strong winds can sway alarmingly. If this happens when the sweet pea tendrils have taken hold, the sweet peas may be torn from the ground. The answer is to knock a short stout stake into the ground inside the spread of the tree and tie one of two branches to it and so prevent them swaying.

Having done that, you will still find that the tips move around a little and sometimes the tendrils fail to get a grip, so they may need a little encouragement and a few gentle ties to send them in the right direction.

PURPLE AND MAUVE Rich purple and mauve are strong and sumptuous colours, and that old stand-by the purple-leaved smokebush again comes into its own as a first-class partner. I also once saw purple sweet peas draped over a huge purple phormium; this was surprising but looked great. Green foliage seems less effective as a support but the silver of sea buckthorn, *Hippophae rhamnoides*, is an excellent companion.

Clematis makes a good partner. The highly scented 'The Doctor' with *Clematis viticella* 'Venosa Violacea' is an enticing prospect, as is 'Blackcurrant Mousse' with 'Madame Edouard André' or the more crimson 'Niobe'. And a white with a touch of darkness would both harmonize and contrast: 'James Mason' with its purple-maroon anthers seems the choice to partner 'Sir Cliff' or 'Bridget'.

LAVENDER This is a classic sweet pea colour and an ideal choice for a large silver-leaved shrub. In mild areas, or on a sheltered west wall in most of Britain, *Acacia baileyana* would be a good choice; its yellow flowers will follow the sweet peas.

Adding scent to *Teucrium fruticans*, whose flowers are lavender, would be an entertaining notion although it is not the most intensely silver of shrubs. So, on balance, one of the silver elaeagnus like *E. angustifolia* would be a good choice as support for 'Ethel Grace' or the lavender and white bicolour 'Dolly Varden'.

Matching with pink roses or pink clematis is another approach. 'Frülingsmorgen' is a single-flowered modern shrub rose in pale rose pink and would be a lovely host for good old favourites 'Leamington' or 'Mrs C. Kay' or the well-scented 'Karen Louise' while, among clematis, the pure white 'Marie Boisselot', with its faint lilac flush on the young flowers, is a good choice as host.

PALE BLUE Pale blue sweet peas like the well-scented 'Cambridge Blue' or the slightly

'Pink Cupid' mingles into the dark-leaved coleus 'Rob Roy' with silvery Pleiostachys serpyllifolia sneaking in from the side.

lavender-tinted 'Charlie's Angel' are good planted under a pale rose like 'New Dawn': the trick is to be sure that the roots of the rose do not suck up all the moisture and nutrients at the expense of the sweet pea – and that some of the rose flowers are carried low down on the plant so that the sweet pea and rose flowers actually mingle; thoughtful pruning is therefore required.

Pale and dark blue sweet peas mixed together also look good, 'Noel Sutton' planted in a ring on a tower of brushwood with 'Cambridge Blue', for example – or with a soft rose-pink variety like 'Anthea Turner'. Or a trio of pale blue 'Honeymoon' or 'Larkspur', the pale rose 'Macmillan Nurse' or 'Southbourne' and white 'Royal Wedding' makes a delightful, highly fragrant group – and so much more dependably effective than a bought mixture.

DARK BLUE Dark blues are relatively few and the old favourite 'Noel Sutton' is only now about to be truly superseded by the impressive, slightly darker and highly scented 'Oxford Blue'. The colour stands out well against the fresh and rich green of a conifer such as *Thuja occidentalis* 'Smaragd', often planted as a hedge, although again water and nutrient requirements must be kept in mind. At least such dense conifers provide plenty of grip for tendrils.

Combine with a really dark clematis like 'Niobe' for a very special rich effect and with *Lavatera* 'Bredon' – the deep rich pink and the dark blue look good. Plant the sweet pea close to the stem of the lavatera, which has been cut back in spring. The lavatera will develop rapidly and the sweet pea will grow through and emerge in flower.

This is the colour, rather than paler blue, with which to compose a patriotic red-white-and-blue blend. Try American grower Pat Sherman's suggestion of 'Fatima', 'White Supreme' and 'Blue Velvet' – or in Grandifloras there's 'Queen Alexandra', 'Valentine' and 'Lord Nelson'.

Mediterranean gardens

Wild annual *Lathyrus* grow naturally in the Mediterranean and so are obvious plants to consider for the Mediterranean-style gardens which, for many people, are a response to the drier summers and milder winters which Britain and other countries are now experiencing. And they're ideal: snaking among shrubs in naturalistic plantings, or grown in more restrained ways in formal arrangements, wild *Lathyrus* are just right.

Lathyrus clymenum 'Articulatus', with its little maroon and white flowers, looks lovely scrambling through mature, blue-silvery *Euphorbia characias* like 'Blue Hills'. The picric yellow flowers of *L. chloranthus* are perfect trailing through the gold-tinted foliage of *Phlomis chrysophylla*. The larger purplish-pink flowers of *L. tingitanus* are good on a fence, perhaps in the background to a Med garden, as is the more prolific *L. chloranthus*.

These species are also very effective tumbling over a wall; this may seem unlikely but once their weight carries them over, more shoots emerge from the base and continue the display; eventually the result is rather a thicket but the flowers just keep coming. Think about the colour of the stone when choosing which species, or variety, to use.

The dainty little *L. sativus*, which develops into a tangled bush rather than climbing like the other species, can also be very pretty in Med situations. The pure blue and the pure white are both effective but you may only be able to buy a mixture – in which case mark the colours in the first year you grow them and collect seed from them for the following year... if you can untangle the stems.

Blue *L. sativus* nestling against the base of *Euphorbia characias* 'Portuguese Velvet' is delightful; a mature plant of the pink-flowered *Lavandula angustifolia* 'Loddon Pink' would also be a good neighbour although a newly planted specimen might be overwhelmed. The white can go around or alongside pink-flowered *Phlomis italica* and will peep through between the branches of a mature plant of *Salvia officinalis* 'Purpurascens' – in fact the blue would also be good with purple-leaved sage.

Summer ground cover

Sweet peas as ground cover, now there's a thought. But a new generation of varieties, or rather the recent expansion in the range of varieties in a very old style, has added this dimension to the many ways in which sweet peas can be grown. Cupid, Sweetie and Pinocchio make excellent neat ground cover which suppresses annual weeds well although more robust perennial weeds will persist.

'Pink Cupid' makes an impressive low carpet about 38–45cm/15–18in across, its tangle of stems topped with pretty bicoloured pink and white flowers. It looks delightful tucked in front of one of the new generation of dark-leaved heucheras such as 'Chocolate Ruffles' and its flowers will peep out among the dark and lustrous foliage.

Similarly, 'Sweetie White' can be tucked in front of a white-edged hosta like 'Francee' and will trail gently over a timber, stone or brick edging and nestle in front of the hosta, ensuring that every speck of soil is covered with greenery. The Sweeties are not solely for hanging baskets.

In annual borders, too, these pretty varieties can provide a more dense cover than alyssum. They are best raised in pots, rather than sown direct, but in front of geraniums, salvias or other relatively upright bedding plants they make great partners.

In summer borders

Intermediate varieties find a happy home as hardy annuals in annual or mixed borders. The problem is finding them in the separate colours required to enable careful planning. Both the Explorer Series and, before them, the Jet Set Series have been used very effectively in this way.

If separate colours again become available, or when using the recent tendril-free Constellation Series, I would suggest raising them in 9cm/3½in pots, planting out the pots 23–30cm/9–12in apart and providing short brushwood to help support them, although this is not strictly necessary. Choose the colours to blend or contrast with their neighbours.

Varieties from the Cupid, Sweetie and Pinocchio series are available to slip into small spaces at the front of borders. 'Pinocchio Red', for example, is attractive peeping out from among the upright stems of *Sedum purdyi* 'Purple Emperor', with its shining deep purple foliage.

Chapter Four
Dwarf sweet peas

Dwarf sweet peas have always excited seed companies and sweet pea breeders; sometimes the gardening public has been equally enthused... though at times they have been noticeably underwhelmed. At the recent turn of the century, a revival of this type began, replicating the enthusiasm that greeted their original introduction over 100 years ago.

In 1893 a startlingly different form of sweet pea was discovered. Among plants of 'Emily Henderson', one of the best whites of the time and derived from 'Blanche Ferry', C. C. Morse & Co. found on their trial ground at Santa Clara, California, a single dwarf plant. Its unusually dwarf character was so fixed that when they grew seven acres of it, not one reverted to the tall type.

Morse sold the variety to Burpee, who sent it to England to be bulked up in Essex. It was shown at the RHS in 1895 and given a unanimous AM. In July 1895 Burpee announced 'Cupid' (with, it should be noted, white flowers). Coincidentally, in Germany, Ernst Benary was poised to introduce exactly the same plant, as 'Tom Thumb White'; however, to avoid confusion, he launched his own discovery under the name 'Cupid'. It would not happen today. In 1895 a similar sport is said to have occurred with Henry Eckford at Wem and possibly also as a sport in 'Old White' in France.

But there was a problem. 'Cupid', later known as 'White Cupid', was white-seeded with the inherent germination problems of this type and in its first year of release it germinated very badly; so its popularity was at once punctured.

A Victorian engraving of 'Cupid' from the time when it was launched.

The uniformity in colour, height, habit and flower production of these 'Pink Cupid', grown for their seed, is impressive.

In 1895 the pink and white bicoloured form, 'Pink Cupid', was found as a sport in 'Blanche Ferry'. Burpee paid $1,500 for the entire stock of 1,068 seeds, surely the highest sum ever paid for a sweet pea, and introduced it in 1898. A "yellow" sport was then found in 'White Cupid' and introduced by Burpee in 1899 as 'Primrose Cupid'.

There was a rush of varieties in the same style in the seven years following the introduction of the original 'White Cupid', and soon all the colours present in the Grandifloras were available in Cupids. It is interesting to note that although some were developed by hybridization, most of the early varieties of this type were found as sports in tall varieties. By 1900 the English nursery of Laxton Brothers in Bedford, who started crossing onto 'Cupid' as soon as it was introduced, were said to have 23 varieties, but it is not clear if all were introduced; the poor germination of the original introduction, coupled with disappointment that these dwarf types did not produce stems long enough for cutting, diminished the popularity of the group. Although 31 varieties are listed as being available in 1912, what popularity there was began to wane.

Robert Sydenham reports, in 1914, that W. Atlee Burpee who introduced the Cupids "fancied that he had found a veritable gold mine, and boomed it hard. A great many seeds were sold, but I rarely hear anyone speak favourably of these Cupids, nor have I fancied them myself, for I have never seen them doing what I consider well, or anything approaching the wonderful illustrations in either the American or English catalogues. They are all very well as curiosities for conservatory decoration, but the stems being so short and the plants not lasting well in bloom I think they will never be popular in England. As a practical proof of this I may say that although I used to put them in my Seed List every year I rarely sold more than about 100 packets, whereas I sell considerably over 500,000 packets of various tall varieties."

In Burpee's *Sweet Peas Up-to-Date* of 1897 there are seven pages of enthusiastic eulogy and refutation of its poor germination qualities. This even included a short verse, originally published in the catalogue of Michael Cuthbertson of Rothesay in Scotland:

"Now 'Cupid' has fluttered from over the sea,
In the form of a charming and lovely Sweet Pea
Six inches in height – stems spreading and low,
With blossoms as white as the beautiful snow."

California grower James T. Lynch said at the time: "As to its blooming qualities, Cupid excels all other Sweet Peas in length of bloom. I have seen it growing all summer along with tall-growing varieties of Sweet Peas, and find that at this late date (17 October, 1896) it is still blooming without irrigation, while other sorts have long been out of bloom. It gives every promise of continuing its season of blooming for a month yet." (Quoted in the 1897 edition of *Sweet Peas Up-to-Date*.)

Sydenham lists 22 Cupids in 1914, including Cupid forms of such popular (and still extant) varieties as 'America', 'Captain of the Blues' and 'Prima Donna'. In 1910 Hursts in Essex received their order of 20kg/43lb of 'Cupid White' and 9kg/20lb of 'Cupid Captain of the Blues' from Morse along with many other colours. However, the true merit of these first Cupids is perhaps revealed by looking at the 1914 edition of Burpee's *Sweet Peas Up-to-Date*, in which only half a page is given over to them. "At one time there was listed fully twenty varieties but now only the following are offered by us: 'Pink Cupid', 'White Cupid', 'Mixed Cupid'."

A similar fall was met with by Burpee's Bush Sweet Peas, said by Burpee to reach 38–45cm/15–18in, and by Sydenham to reach 90cm/3ft in 1914 when he said: "This group we certainly hoped to be the forerunners of an entirely new and distinct race," and suggests 20 different varieties (many, again, versions of popular tall varieties) but goes on to say: "I cannot recommend them with any confidence or pleasure." In another disappointment for Mr Burpee, his 1914 *Sweet Peas Up-to-Date* regrets: "As these have not met with the success anticipated they have been discarded." And that, you might think, was that. Far from it.

With the tendency to ever-smaller gardens and the reluctance of many weekend gardeners to bother with supports and tying in, Dwarf and Intermediate sweet peas have regularly been revived. The Cupids reappeared in the 1950s, winning ten RHS awards, but soon faded again. In the 1960s and 1970s, Ferry–Morse, Denholm, and Burpee in the USA worked on Intermediates of various sorts. The highly scented Jet Sets, from Ferry–Morse, won many RHS awards as did their surprisingly tall Knee-Hi series, originally growing over 1.5m/5ft tall. It is strange now to see at least one seed company listing 'Knee

Hi' as a synonym for 'Jet Set'. Other award-winning names of this period included the Elf, California and Americana series.

At about the same time, E. W. King launched its very successful Snoopea Intermediate tendril-free type, and this was followed soon after by the earlier-flowering Supersnoops from Denholm in the USA.

Over the years a number of Dwarf and Intermediate types have appeared, including Patio, Bijou, Little Sweetheart, Continental, but they have never enjoyed huge popularity and, at the same time, the previously superb Jet Sets have declined from a series of over 20 separate colours to an unpredictable mixture.

In recent years, however, there has been another revival. 'Pink Cupid', sent by a customer to Hursts, who had also worked on this group and held a huge trial in 1902, was bulked up, launched, faded, then relaunched to become widely available as plants in garden centres for use in patio pots. Tony Hender has revived a wider range of colours, now up to 11, and the most suitable of this group for use as hanging basket plants, have been selected for the Sweetie Series. Andrew Beane, raiser of a number of excellent Spencer types, has also worked on this group, and his Pinocchio Series, with more of an emphasis on striped flowers, is also worth growing. Others are also working on Dwarf types.

In the Intermediates, the tendril-free Explorer Series repeated the success of the Jet Sets in Wisley trials, with awards for many of its colours, and was spectacular both on the trials field and in gardens; however, this has quickly faded and now, sadly, exists almost exclusively as a mixture. Now, Kings, who raised Snoopea, the original tendril-free bush type, have revisited this area and launched their New Century Constellation Series, one of which, 'Virgo', has the unique distinction of winning an AM for exhibition.

Unwins, too, have introduced an Intermediate type. 'Minuet', reaching about 3ft/90cm, is a pretty, sparkling mix of stripes but the separate colours are, unfortunately, not available. This is an excellent container plant.

Chapter Five
Sweet peas in containers

Sweet peas are surprisingly amenable to being grown in containers. True, the size of the container must suit the type of sweet pea with which it is planted, but containers provide relatively untapped potential for some delightful garden features and associations.

Sweet peas in tubs

Until recently sweet peas have been seen only in the largest tubs – half barrels and large stone and terracotta pots – and often only in the largest gardens, but things are changing. The increasing availability of large terracotta pots at a modest price and the widespread retailing of surprisingly elegant large plastic pots have encouraged gardeners other than those in stately homes to plant containers on a large scale. This suits sweet peas, as they appreciate the more extensive root run, and the availability of patio watering kits has helped ensure that they can have access to all the moisture they need. Garden centres and garden shops nowadays stock elegant steel or woven hazel and birch supports for climbers which enables design-conscious gardeners to avoid using an obtrusive wigwam of bamboo canes in a container. The featuring of 'Cupani' as a container-grown specimen in full flower at the Chelsea Flower Show in recent years has also alerted gardeners to the appeal of growing sweet peas in this way.

It is also possible to grow the climbing types as trailing varieties on balconies and over the edge of raised terraces. They should be planted in large tubs, but without supports – although it has been suggested that short supports be used initially. Once the plants are growing well, they are simply pushed over one side of the pot. They will continue to grow as they trail down wildly, and flower, as new shoots arise from the base to continue the display. This is a technique which was first suggested 100 years ago but is rarely seen. There are, of course, relatively few situations in which it is appropriate – strong winds being the chief enemy – but the waterfall of colour it can create is worth the gamble.

The compost for use in tubs should preferably be soil-based (look for John Innes No 3 in Britain) as this will hold more nutrients for the full length of the season. If it is necessary to use peat-based mixes, add 25 per cent by volume of extra drainage material in the form of sharp grit. Grit is preferable to the much lighter perlite as the extra weight in otherwise lightweight compost will help counterbalance the tall and heavy top growth.

'Matucana' growing on canes in a vivid matching timber pot on a wooden decking patio.

Planting technique varies according to the size of the tub. When using smaller tubs, 30–35cm/12–14in, a 12.5cm/5in pot of six pinched seedlings can be planted in the centre and the shoots guided to the supports and tied in; once the shoots are on their correct route up the supports they will usually cling, though they may need help as they approach the top.

For the preferable larger containers, which will always provide a more effective and longer-lasting display, it is probably wiser to plant seedlings grown in Rootrainers as individuals alongside supports or to separate seedlings grown together in pots for individual plantings. This will give their roots speedier access to more compost and each plant will have its own support.

Regular feeding and watering are essential. A drip system of watering which can be turned on easily is ideal, and the weekly use of a balanced (rather than a high nitrogen) liquid feed will help keep growth sturdy and flower production continuous. Dead-heading is essential not only to improve the appearance but to ensure consistent flower production.

Most climbing varieties, Grandifloras and Spencers, are suitable for large containers but species, such as *L. chloranthus* and *L. tingitanus*, tend to produce so much growth that the structure becomes unwieldy and the effect inelegant. However, given that most will be viewed at close quarters, those varieties with a delicate patterning of colour, which is less visible from the greater distance at which flowers are seen in a border, and those with scent, are the most suitable.

Picotees are especially appealing. Try the white 'Anniversary' with its pink edge and 'Mollie Rilstone' in rich cream with a pink border. Those with a subtle combination of colours like 'Anthea Turner', a soft meld of cream and pink, 'Appleblossom' with its haze of rose pink on white and 'Rosy Frills' with its bolder pink picotee look superb and are well scented.

Striped varieties with their intricate pattern of colouring are also very effective in close-up, some of the best also being well scented. 'Nimbus', with its unique blue-black markings, 'Aquarius' in soft blue and 'Pulsar' in a strong mauve are all fragrant. Grandifloras almost always provide fragrance, and

'Pink Cupid' growing in a container with the delightful seed-raised Viola 'Magnifico'.

the opportunity to appreciate this, and their generally rather smaller flowers, make them good candidates. The old flakes like 'America', red on white, 'Senator', purple on white, 'Kingfisher', dark blue on white, are fine choices, as are those in softer shades like the soft pink 'Prima Donna' or the bolder bicolour of 'Cupani'.

Modern Grandifloras with a subtlety of colouring are also ideal tub varieties. The exquisite 'Romeo', with its powerful fragrance and an edge of purple wire to the white flower, and the beigey-pink 'Juliet' both repay close inspection.

An entirely different approach, and one which works especially well on small town patios, is to grow the Dwarf varieties as specimens in 30cm/12in terracotta pots. Making a low, often fragrant dome of foliage and flower, which trails neatly over the sides of the pot, they flower for weeks – often without the necessity even for dead-heading. Use a soil-based compost if possible and plant three seedlings in the centre of each pot. It is essential to keep them consistently moist and fed regularly to maintain the succession of flowers but the long-lasting summer display will be very rewarding. These Dwarf types sometimes take a pause in flowering in midsummer, but fresh new shoots carrying the next phase of flower buds are to be seen already emerging.

The Pinocchio Series, with its preponderance of prettily patterned striped flowers, is especially well suited to this approach while 'Pink Cupid', a pink and white bicolour, is particularly pretty and the best scented of the Cupid Series.

Hanging baskets and window boxes

Growing sweet peas in hanging baskets is not a notion which immediately leaps to the mind of most gardeners but with the revival of Dwarf types this is now completely feasible. And we would all be grateful for a viable, not to say fragrant, alternative to the omnipresent petunia. Two series are especially suitable: the Sweeties and the Pinocchios plus the delightful 'Balcony Bride'.

Try to choose as large a basket as possible to give the plants the root space they need, a diameter of 30cm/12in at the very minimum. Baskets vary, not only in their width, but also in their depth, so choose the deepest. Again, a soil-based compost is preferable, but weight is often a factor in deciding on the compost for baskets so a peat- or coir- based compost with the addition of perlite to enhance the drainage is helpful. It is essential to keep the compost moist and to feed regularly.

Choosing companions for these dwarfs requires a little thought. Most neither trail as long as many petunias nor billow out so bushily as trailing lobelias. The exception is 'Balcony Bride', a very pretty soft pink stripe which is bushy enough to make a happy intermingler with a pale blue trailing lobelia like 'Blue Cascade' or the blue and white bicoloured *Lobelia* 'Regatta Blue Splash'.

Most require neater companions. *Helichrysum petiolare* 'Goring Silver' is ideal, being much less vigorous than the more familiar helichrysum varieties with their long trails. It looks good with both pastel and richer shades; curly parsley is also a good foliage partner.

To bring in colours other than those available in dwarf sweet peas, consider these plants, which are in roughly the right scale: *Anagallis* 'Skylover' with small brilliant blue flowers, *Brachyscome* 'Lemon Mist' and the mauve *B. multifida*, the neat blue *Scaevola* 'Saphira', *Callibrachoa* 'Million Bells Lemon' (not the trailing Million Bells types which hang down in too much of a curtain), the yellow trailing antirrhinums, lantanas (in particular the white form with a yellow eye) and suteras in the newer fiery shades.

Another approach is to grow them without companions, either in single colours or in a carefully selected blend of separate colours. 'Pink Cupid', 'White Cupid' and 'Rose Cupid', for example, would make an attractive partnership.

Chapter Six
Classification of sweet peas

Some of the terms used in the classification of sweet peas, either by their general type or by their flower type, require explanation.

TYPES OF PLANT

Species *Lathyrus* found growing in the wild. Our cultivated sweet peas are all developed from *L. odoratus* although a number of other annual species are grown including *L. clymenum*, *L. sativus*, *L. tingitanus*, etc. (page 97).

Originals The few forms, developed from the species, which were grown before the rapid development of the Grandifloras.

Grandiflora The first major improvements in sweet peas, with larger flowers, improved placement of the

petals, with the standards held more vertically and with the wings held more evenly. Grandifloras also generally feature clearer colours and more flowers on a stem than their few predecessors, which were selections derived from the first introduction from Sicily. Most Grandifloras are also well scented. The main raisers were Henry Eckford in Britain and C. C. Morse & Co. and W. Atlee Burpee in California, although many other breeders raised their own varieties, most of which have disappeared. Peter Grayson, E. W. King & Co. and Unwins Seeds are now again working in this group, developing new varieties in the same style.

It is perhaps worth stating here that the forms of the old Grandifloras that we grow today are not necessarily identical to those which were grown 100 years ago. Some are, but some have disappeared and then been "rediscovered", perhaps as reversions in Spencer types or in other Grandifloras. Although these may be very similar in flower colour, they may also be more vigorous, their flowers may be larger and they may carry more flowers on a stem.

It is also clear from the old literature that many Grandifloras were not fixed when released, some accounts going so far as to list the names of the other varieties which appeared as rogues in a particular variety. This is a problem found in other old-fashioned plants which are undergoing a revival, particularly pinks and old primroses. Another surprising fact is that in the early development of the Spencers, when one was released that was the same colour as an existing Grandiflora, it tended to borrow the Grandiflora's name – 'Flora Norton Spencer', for example. So it is wise to be aware that what we grow today may not be exactly the same as was grown under the same name 100 or 200 years ago.

'Explorer Mixed' on trial at the RHS Garden at Wisley, with the trial of Spencer varieties in the background.

'Cuthbertson Mixed'

Old-fashioned Sometimes used as a synonym for Grandiflora, but also used to include 'Cupani' and the very first varieties before the explosion of Grandiflora introductions.

Unwins Type One of the first breakthroughs from the Grandifloras and intermediate between Grandifloras and Spencers in both size of flower and degree of ruffling. The term soon fell out of use as Charles Unwin himself developed his new varieties more in the style of 'Countess Spencer'. Although less dramatically ruffled and waved than the Spencer sweet peas, the Unwins Type had the enormous advantage of being largely true to type as a result of the more painstaking work of Charles Unwin in ensuring that his seed contained no off types. He soon brought this consistency to his own range of varieties of the Spencer type.

Spencer Most sweet peas that we grow in the early twenty-first century fall into this group. Discovered by a number of people (page 9), the biggest stir was caused by the variety 'Countess Spencer', shown by Silas Cole, gardener at Althorp Hall in Northamptonshire. The flowers are significantly larger than those of the Grandifloras from which they developed and the petals are noticeably ruffled and waved. They require 12-hour days to flower so are later than Cuthbertsons and Winter-Flowering types. Also sometimes known as Late Spencers, especially in the USA.

Cuthbertson Bred in California by the Ferry–Morse Seed Company from Spencers and an early-flowering American strain, the Cuthbertsons flower two weeks before the Spencer types, in 11-hour days, and are also better able to withstand high summer temperatures. Sometimes grown under glass for cut flowers in Britain, they often carry four to six flowers per stem but the colour range is limited and the flower form less impressive than that of the Spencers. In recent years stocks have deteriorated so that growers often find that their Cuthbertsons may not, in fact, flower much earlier than their Spencers. Sometimes known as Cuthbertson's Floribundas.

Galaxy Flowering at about the same time as the Spencers, the Galaxy sweet peas have up to eight, or more, flowers on a stem but without the ruffled Spencer flower form. In the 1970s there was a feeling that they might supersede the Spencers, but this has never happened.

Multiflora/Semi-multiflora The distinction between these groups is a little unclear; suffice it to say that modern varieties, usually called Semi-multifloras, have five to seven flowers per stem, usually in the waved Spencer form. With classic Spencers often now boasting five flowers per stem the distinction is rather vague.

Dwarf Growing no more than about 30cm/12in high, at first these appeared unexpectedly as rogues in batches of other varieties grown for seed. The first, 'Cupid', was white, then other colours appeared and were introduced (page 27) but they fell out of favour for decades. All are so low and short-stemmed that their main value is as annual ground cover, and in window boxes and hanging baskets. Some are scented. Now breeders are again working in this group and 'Pink Cupid' has become a widespread garden-centre plant. In addition to the Cupid Series other names associated with this group include Patio, Fantasia, Little Sweetheart, Colour Carpet, Sweetie and Pinocchio.

Intermediate Originally developed mainly in the USA by crossing Dwarf types and Spencers, Bijou grows to about 60cm/2ft while Knee-Hi, Jet-Set and Continental are a little taller at about 90cm/3ft. Also known as Semi-dwarf. The tendril-free Snoopea, Supersnoop, Explorer and New Century Constellation series also fall into this category.

Early or Winter-Flowering Developed to flower quickly, and requiring just ten hours of daylight to bloom, these are intended for areas where summers are too hot for other types; they are at their best before the summer heat becomes too overpowering. The Winter Elegance Series is the most widely grown example.

Early Multiflora Giganteas These are earlier than Spencers and are popular with commercial cut-flower growers for their large, good-quality flowers on long stems. The Mammoth Series is a longer-stemmed,

A   'Nimbus'
B   'Solway Sunset'
C   'Kyle the Clown'
D   'Tom'
E   'Candy'
F   'Darcey Bussell'
G   'Mars'
H   'Aquarius'

larger-flowered development which is also more uniform in its flowering time across the colours.

Acacia-leaved Instead of tendrils, these unusual sweet peas have slender, acacia-like foliage. Three Intermediate types are the most often seen – Snoopea, Supersnoop and Explorer, together with the relatively new New Century Constellation. The lack of tendrils is much less of a disadvantage to short-growing types than it is on a tall type which would expect to use its tendrils for support. Tall tendril-free types have occasionally been introduced, but were never a great success. More recently the tendril-free 'Astronaut' mixture with Spencer-type flowers has been introduced by Thompson & Morgan.

Royals An improved form of the Cuthbertsons, also from Ferry–Morse, their stems are longer and stronger, the plants more vigorous and the flowers larger although also later flowering. They are also more tolerant of hot and bright summer weather than the better-known Spencer types.

'Mars', a striped variety, and 'Oklahoma', a flake (below), to highlight the distinction.

Types of flowers

Self In selfs, the flower colour is more or less uniform across the whole flower, both standards and wings.

Bicolour The standard, the upper part of the flower, is a different colour from the wings or a darker version of the same colour; the clearer the distinction between the two colours the more effective and dramatic the flower.

Reverse Bicolours Here, the standards are a paler shade than the wings.

Flake A boldly patterned type in which both standards and wings are streaked in, usually, a dark colour on a white or grey-white background. The reverses of both standards and wings are very similar to the front although often more intensely coloured; 'America' is an early Grandiflora in this style.

Stripe Dramatically marked, the flowers are usually white, or close to white, and patterned in a very striking way. The standards are edged with a narrow band of colour, the remainder of the petal being usually almost uncoloured; on the reverse there is heavy colouring, with a narrow uncoloured zone between the coloured zone and a narrow coloured rim. The wings are very similar to the standards – but in reverse. So on the upper surface the wings are strongly coloured, with a narrow uncoloured zone immediately inside the coloured wired rim; the edges which face each other over the keel are also more broadly coloured. Underneath, the wings are more or less white, with the edges wired in colour. The heavy colour on one side dulls the purity of the whiteness when seen from the other. 'Wiltshire Ripple' is a familiar example. The terms 'stripe' and 'flake' were once used more loosely than today.

Marble Rarely seen form in which the colour occurs in the veins of the petals.

Picotee Picotees have a narrow border along the edge of the petals which is a darker shade of, and often a noticeable contrast to, the main petal colour. 'Rosy Frills' is a familiar example.

Chapter Seven
The sweet peas: descriptions

Describing sweet peas is not easy. This might seem, at first glance, to be a neat alphabetical list of varieties systematically described, but it is not quite that. There are a number of problems that make the results variable and subjective. First of all, the exact way in which the petals are held, and the degree of waviness, can vary with the way they are grown, the state of the plants (dry, moist; peak season, late season) and the time of day at which they are inspected. The same flower on the same plant may look different on two consecutive days. Many of the flowers from which my descriptions were made were grown naturally, in England, but some were seen only on cordons, a few only at shows and some in the United States. Many older varieties, some less significant varieties, and some that I was unable to see in the summer in which I compiled this information, have a shorter and less detailed description and rely upon the descriptions of others. So not only are sweet pea flowers variable, but so are these descriptions.

The descriptions of many older varieties are in the form of quotations from contemporary accounts, in particular the extensive catalogue and descriptive list of all available sweet peas by Robert Sydenham (noted as RS) published in 1914, and from *Sweet Peas Up-To-Date* by G. W. Kerr (GWK), also published in 1914, an earlier edition of this book, by Reverend W. T. Hutchins (WTH), published in 1897, and *Field Notes on Sweet Peas* (1916), edited by Lester Morse (LM). These reveal the features of the varieties as they were originally grown. A century later, the few varieties we still grow may have altered as a result of genetic drift and selection by gardeners in different parts of the world. Some descriptions are based on those of the raisers or those published in association with the invaluable long-running RHS trials at Wisley in Surrey.

Then there is the minefield of colour. We all think we know what we mean by 'red', or 'pink', yet both cover a range of shades – so I have tried to be more precise. In particular, many catalogues use the term 'salmon'. There are many shades that could be so described, and so I have tried to use the term as little as possible, and mainly when following contemporary descriptions of older varieties I have not recently seen. So the colour descriptions are as I saw them on the day, or days, when I inspected the variety in question. I have included a note of the bud colour and keel colour only when I found it especially noteworthy but not otherwise.

I have given each sweet pea its category – Spencer, Original, Grandiflora, Modern Grandiflora, Dwarf, Intermediate – but not distinguished between Spencers of different heights; height can vary enormously according to the conditions in which they are being grown. The distinction between Spencers and Grandifloras is also sometimes less than obvious, both for early so-called Spencer varieties and more recent introductions; some varieties with large Spencer-sized flowers are almost unwaved, while some with smaller, Grandiflora-sized flowers show a noticeable waviness. And this, too, unfortunately, can vary with the conditions. The term Semi-Grandiflora is occasionally used and refers to varieties between Grandifloras and Spencers in flower size.

In the early years of this century, new Spencer varieties in the same colour as previous Grandifloras were often simply given a modified version of the Grandiflora name, e.g. 'Flora Norton Spencer' is the same colour as 'Flora Norton' but in the waved Spencer form. This is confusing and may be one reason why contemporary plants grown under old Grandiflora names sometimes seem a little too good to be true. This practice also extended to the Cupid types and Bush types. So in 1914 the variety 'America' was available, together with 'America Spencer', an 'America' of the Cupid type and also an 'America' in the Bush type growing about 90cm/3ft tall. This seems very confusing by contemporary standards of nomenclature.

A   *'Rosy Frills'*
B   *'Royal Baby'*
C   *'Sally Ann'*
D   *'Charlie's Angel'*
E   *'Cream Southbourne'*
F   *'Restormel'*
G   *'Ken Colledge'*

I have also noted where the variety has received the Award of Garden Merit from the Royal Horticultural Society, using the increasingly familiar cup symbol. ♛ This is the most useful award for gardeners, indicating true excellence as a garden plant. At the end of each entry, where possible, I have noted the raiser and the year of introduction. This information is far from complete and I would appreciate any additional details via the sweet peas website at www.scentedsweetpeas.co.uk.

Fragrance is another important factor, and obviously has a prejudicial subjectivity until the unlikely event of someone scientifically analysing each variety. I have graded each variety according to the power of its scent: strongly scented, well scented, slightly scented and hardly scented – no sweet pea is entirely unscented. These are based on a variety of sources including personal experience, raisers' descriptions, trials notes, books and personal accounts. If there is no mention of degree of fragrance, this indicates that I was unable to sniff it myself and no one else has thought to indicate if the scent is especially weak or strong.

The varieties I have chosen for inclusion in this list include almost all those available to gardeners in the UK or USA at the time of writing.

DESCRIPTIONS

'Aerospace' (Spencer)
White, with well-waved standards and wings, the wings spreading. Well scented. (Manning)

'Air Force' (Spencer)
Misty blue. Well scented. (Grayson, 1997)

'Air Warden' (Spencer)
Prolific brilliant scarlet cerise. Well scented.

'Alan Titchmarsh' (Spencer)
Slightly two-tone rich sugar pink. Standards pale rose, merging to cream at the base; wings slightly darker and pale rose at the rim, the rest of the wings deeper and richer. Good strong grower. Especially good for cutting. Named for the TV presenter in 1985. Well scented. (Bolton)

'Alan Williams' (Spencer)
Very slightly two-tone blue. Standards mauve, pale at the edges, rolled back, with a small white mark at the base which is delicately whiskered in purple. Wings more blue, slightly silvered, pale at the edges, nicely rippled. Strongly scented. (Williams)

'Alaska Blue' (Spencer) ♛ 2000
Very pretty pale ice blue. Both the waved standards and the waved spreading wings are white, flushed with blue, giving an attractive ice blue effect. Vigorous. Strongly scented. (Wells, 2000) There was once also a pure white 'Alaska'. (Burpee)

'Alastair' (Spencer)
A very prolific, glowing cherry red, almost maroon. Intended for exhibition. Hardly scented. (Unwins, 1988)

'Albutt Blue' (Spencer)
Very pretty, purple-blue picotee. Standards gently but evenly waved; white, with purple whiskers at the base, and a pretty, slender, purple-blue picotee; reverse, slightly more coloured. Wings white, with a similar, narrow, purple-blue picotee; reverse paler. Heads rather tightly clustered with three to four flowers. A great garden variety although the flowers are small. Strongly scented. (Albutt)

'Alica' (Spencer)
Pale rose and cream. Small flowers, hardly waved. Standards hazy rose, cream at the base and creamier on the reverse; paling with age but retaining a creamy centre; gently waved. Wings neatly peaked over the keel, same hazy rose. Neat and pretty but small-flowered.

'Alice Hardwicke' (Spencer)
Long-stemmed rosy salmon. Well scented.

'America' (Grandiflora) ♛ 1995
A sparkling red flake. Standards upright, flat, rounded at the top and peaked; white with vermilion streaks; reverse more densely coloured, especially at the top.

'America'

'Angela Ann'

Wings similar but coloured slightly more purple, angled down around keel and rolled in, paler below. Usually three flowers per stem. Sometimes includes red/purple bicoloured rogues. "One of the four best and brightest for those who liked striped varieties." (RS) Strongly scented. (Morse, 1896) There was also an 'America Spencer', "A grand variety, like 'America', but of fine 'Countess Spencer' type, and very large flowers, generally four on a stem." (RS) (Stevenson, 1908)

'Andrea Robertson' (Spencer)
Midnight blue. (2000)

'Andrew Unwin' (Spencer)
Large, long-stemmed flowers in an unusual pale blue tinted with soft lavender grey. The last variety raised by Charles Unwin. Strongly scented. (Unwins, 1989)

'Angela Ann' (Spencer)
Late flowering, pretty almond pink on white. Standards open sugary rose, cream at the edge, paling towards the base, with the edges rolled forward; hardly waved. They develop to being broadly waved, white at the

base, then more or less uniform sugary pink, white showing through. Wings open dark, not cream, paler below, then pink veins develop on a white ground. Elegant eventually; finally whole flower fades slightly. Good exhibition variety. Well scented. (Albutt)

'Angel's Blush' (Dwarf)
Large almond-pink blooms. Slightly trailing habit. Well scented.

'Annabelle' (Spencer)
Long-stemmed clear bright lavender, frilly flowers. Prolific and good for exhibition and garden decoration. Good in bad weather. Well scented. (Bolton)

'Anne Barron' (Spencer)
Well-frilled flowers in soft pink overlaying a rich cream background. Prolific and easy to grow. Good for both garden and exhibition.

'Anne Gregg' (Spencer)
Rich cream with frilly flowers. Named for the TV presenter. Well scented.

A *'Isabella Cochrane'*
B *'Emma'*
C *'Macmillan Nurse'*
D *'Norman Wisdom'*
E *'Daphne'*
F *'Appleblossom'*
G *'Honey Pink'*

'Anne Vestry' (Spencer)
Bright cerise.

'Annie B. Gilroy' (Grandiflora)
"Bright carmine pink standard, pale pink wings... usually three flowers on a stem." (RS) "A deep cerise of poor form." (LM) (Eckford, 1907)

'Annie Good' (Spencer)
Bright carmine with a white eye. Standards broadly waved, carmine with a white eye. Wings same colour, broadly and evenly waved. Hardly scented. (Tasker)

'Anniversary' (Spencer)
Gorgeous pink picotee. Opens very creamy with a pink edge. Develops well-ruffled, reflexed standards in sharp white, with a broad rose pink band at the edge; reverse darker. Wings waved, a slightly less pure white with a hint of pink at the edge. Beautiful garden variety, superb for exhibition and familiar at top flower shows. Strongly scented.

'Anthea Turner' (Spencer)
Rippled, soft sugar pink flowers shading to slightly creamy white at the centre. Named for the TV presenter. Strongly scented.

'Antique Fantasy' (Grandiflora)
One of many names for mixtures of Grandiflora varieties. Strongly scented.

'Appeal' (Spencer)
Cerise with salmon tints. Well scented.

'Appleblossom' (Spencer)
A very pretty, delicately rose pink, striped variety. Standards white, edges rolled back or sometimes rolled forward and noticeably well ruffled, flushed with rose pink, with a slightly cerise tint towards the centre; reverse white with a slightly stronger haze of pink in the centre. Wings ruffled, rolled down at the edges, white with a rose pink band either side of the keel and a haze of pink in the centre of each petal, more or less white below. Very pretty from distance, but a little muddled from close to. In effect, a pale pink stripe. Relatively late into flower; some duplex flowers. Slightly scented. (2001) There was once also: 'Apple Blossom', a pink and white Grandiflora with four flowers per stem, and one of Henry Eckford's first in 1887; 'Apple Blossom Spencer' (also known as 'Apple Blossom Waved'), from Burpee in 1908, described as "very much in the way of 'Mrs A. Ireland' (one of the few to receive an FCC in 1908)... too near to warrant another name". (RS)

'Appleblossom Pink' (Spencer)
Pink standards with lavender-tinted pink wings. (2001)

'Apricot Queen' (Spencer) ♛ 1994
A paler, more gentle version of 'Queen Mother'. Soft pale orange, not really apricot. Strongly scented. (King)

'Apricot Sprite' (Modern Grandiflora)
Strong peachy orange standards and bright pink falls. Well scented. (Thompson & Morgan, 2002)

'April in Paris' (Spencer)
Large, well-waved flowers in pale cream, with a deepening lilac flush. Strongly scented. (2002)

'Aquarius' (Spencer)
Pretty dark lavender blue stripe. Standards upright, waved but rolled back strongly and sometimes rolled forward at the edge; white, with a dark lavender blue central vertical stripe and a slight dusting of gentle denim blue flecks in a radiating pattern; reverse mostly lavender blue, creamy white at the base and sides. Wings white at the base, solid pale lavender blue along the edges above the keel, then a fairly solid zone of lavender blue becoming less dense towards the edge, then solidifying to provide a neat border. No clear white zone between the edge and the body colour. Tending to roll back at the sides or edges, but nicely waved. Has the look of an intermediate between Grandiflora and Spencer types. Sometimes rather late; some duplex flowers. Excellent for cutting or in the garden. (Place, 2001) There is also an 'Aquarius' in the Intermediate New Century Constellation Series.

'Arbor Low' (Spencer)
Cerise pink. Strongly scented. (Albutt)

'Argirina' (Dwarf) 🏆 2000
Pretty, very dwarf carmine and white bicolour. Standards pale carmine on the front, the edge rolled forward; reverse darker. Wings both front and reverse white with a hint of carmine with the edge rolled down. The whole flower pales noticeably with age, the standards become white with a few pale carmine streaks. Good dwarf garden variety.

'Arley Hall'
An unremarkable blue. Named for the famous garden at Arley Hall in Cheshire where it has been grown for many years.

'Arthur Hellyer' (Spencer)
Very pretty pale lavender. Standards upright, boldly waved, though occasionally not waved, sometimes rolled back at the edge; white at the base, then with broad hazy lavender zone and then white again at the edge though with a creamy margin at the top; reverse paler. Wings as standards, but the lavender colour runs right to the edge. Good in the garden, for exhibition and for cutting. Well scented. (Francis)

'Ascot' (Spencer)
Light salmon pink. (Unwins, 1981)

'Astronaut' (Spencer)
Tall, tendril-free plants with exhibition-quality flowers in red, pinks and pink flushes, blue, lavender and white. (Thompson & Morgan, 2002)

'Auntie Molly' (Spencer)
Pretty soft carmine flowers open from bright cream and pink buds. Good for cottagey borders. Slightly scented. (Unwins, 2002)

'Aunt Jane' (Spencer) 🏆 1997
Standards very ruffled, strongly reflexed; densely veined rose carmine, white at the base; the reverse silvery rose mauve. Wings more solid in colour, slightly pale at the edges, paler below. Especially good in the garden on a pyramid. Named for David Matthewman's favourite aunt. Strong scent. (Matthewman)

'Avon Beauty' (Spencer)
Deep lavender.

'Balcony Bride' (Dwarf/Intermediate)
A very pretty, prolific and tough soft pink stripe intended for baskets and window boxes.

'Ballerina' (Spencer)
Deep cream with a wide deep pink picotee edge. Strongly scented. (Unwins, 1960)

'Balmoral' (Spencer)
Maroon with purple highlights.

'Band Aid' (Spencer)
Soft salmon pink on cream. Strongly scented. (Unwins, 1987)

'Baronscourt' (Spencer)
Rich mauve, recommended for exhibition. Strongly scented.

'Barry Dare' (Spencer)
Noticeably good deep scarlet. Standards deep scarlet, almost cherry red, slightly paler at the lobes; more cerise on opening and paler at the lobes; waved rather than ruffled. Wings strongly rippled, deep scarlet with slightly more cerise tint and paler below. Keel strongly coloured. Stronger colour than many so-called scarlets which seem slightly orange-tinted. Long stout stems, good for cutting and exhibition. Named for the former Managing Director of Unwins Seeds. (Unwins)

'Batheaston' (Spencer)
Large flowered pale pink on a white ground. Well scented.

'Beacon' (Spencer)
Scarlet. (Unwins, 1979) There was also a Grandiflora 'Beacon' described as "Hardly worth

'Blue Danube'

mentioning" (RS) – and not mentioned by GWK! But LN says: "Standard carmine, wings clear primrose... an improvement on 'Duke of York'.!" (Bolton, 1906)

'Beaujolais' (Spencer)
Large-flowered, deep burgundy maroon. Introduced as 'Sutton's Beaujolais'. Well scented.

'Beautiful Blues' (Spencer)
A delightful selection of blues and lavenders.

'Beauty Queen' (Spencer)
Salmon pink.

'Benjamin Townsend' (Modern Grandiflora)
White. Strongly scented. (Grayson)

'Bert Boucher' (Spencer) 🏆 1997
Highly fragrant white. Both standards and wings well waved. Recommended for garden and exhibition. Strongly scented. (Boucher)

'Bicolour Melody' (Spencer)
See 'Melody', page 72.

'Bijou' (Dwarf)
Early-flowering mix of ruffled types in red, salmon, blue, rose, lilac and pink. When well grown, the stems are just long enough for cutting. Needs watering and feeding to provide a long display and long stems. Slightly scented.

'Bishop's Rock' (Spencer) 🏆 1996
Vivid purple violet. Well scented. (Albutt)

'Blackcurrant Mousse' (Spencer)
Purple-flushed mauve. (1999)

'Black Diamond' (Spencer)
Dark maroon.

'Black Knight' (Grandiflora)
"Bold, upright dark bronzey chocolate standard; some say shiny marone, wings a little more purple...; one of the best, if not the best, of all the very dark varieties of the old type." (RS) Strongly scented. (Eckford, 1898) There was also a Spencer version of 'Black Knight' called 'Black Knight Spencer' described as "the very best of the dark Spencer varieties". (RS)

'Black Prince' (Spencer)
Dark, velvety maroon; one of the most black. Well scented. (Unwins, 1975) There was also a previous Grandiflora of this name, said at its release (1910) to be "only a selection from 'Black Knight' ". (RS) Introduced by Kelways, but not listed by 1912!

'Blanche Ferry' (Grandiflora)
"Pale rosy standard and white wings; quite distinct...; a great improvement on the old 'Painted

'Borderline'

Lady', and forces well, coming into bloom twelve to fourteen days earlier than the ordinary varieties." (RS) (Page 8.) Named for the daughter of the founder of D. M. Ferry & Co. (Ferry, 1889)

'Blaze' (Spencer)
Dazzling deep orange with overtones of scarlet. Sun-proof. Well scented. (Unwins, 1974)

'Blondel' (Spencer)
Large-flowered cream. (F. Woodcock)

'Blue Danube' (Spencer)
Large, frilly, deep blue flowers on long stems. Vigorous, and good for the garden and exhibition. Strongly scented. (Unwins, 1981)

'Blue Flake' (Spencer)
Deep blue stripes and a blue-tinted white background.

'Blue Ice' (Spencer)
Waved standards, lightly tinted blue, paling towards the edge; wings waved, colour as standards. Well scented. (Colledge) There was also an earlier 'Blue Ice'. (Unwins, 1949)

'Blue Mantle' (Spencer)
Unusually vigorous deep violet blue. Well scented. (Unwins, 1977)

'Blue Reflections' (Spencer)
Soft lavenders, blues, violets and maroons in selfs and bicolours. Strongly scented. (Hammett, 2002)

'Blue Riband' (Spencer)
Mid blue. (Unwins, 1971)

'Blue Ripple' (Spencer)
Frilly flowers, white with blue flecks. Slightly scented.

'Blue Triumph' (Spencer)
Large-flowered and vigorous, rich, deep blue. Strongly scented. (Bolton)

'Blue Velvet' (Spencer)
Long-stemmed, well-ruffled, very deep blue. (Unwins, 1972)

'Blushing Bride' (Spencer)
Palest of soft pink on cream. (King)

'Bobby's Girl' (Spencer) 🏆 2000
An impressive salmon-cream. A very productive and large-flowered variety, many stems boast five flowers; both the waved standards and the spreading waved wings are cream flushed with salmon. Strongly scented. (Bolton, 2000)

'Borderline' (Spencer) 🏆 1994
White, streaked and flushed with strong reddish-purple. Vigorous. Strongly scented. (Albutt)

Bouquet Series
Bred particularly for its exceptional vigour, excellent productivity, stronger than usual flower stems, and large flowers – well scented in many of the colours. The eight colours are: Rose, Pink, Lavender, Navy, White, Scarlet, Mid Blue and Salmon Cream Pink. Unfortunately, only the mixture is now usual-

A   'Midnight'
B   'Heathcliff'
C   'Sylvia'
D   'Linda C'
E   'Angela Ann'
F   'Vera Lynn'
G   'Miranda Crafer'

ly available. There was also a mauve Spencer 'Bouquet'. (Unwins, 1962)

'Bowhouse' (Spencer)
Large-flowered, mauve with flowers well waved on strong stems. Slightly scented.

'Brian Clough' (Spencer)
Excellent bright scarlet rose. Standards upright, nicely waved, scarlet rose, darkest in the centre, paler at the edges and base; reverse rather misty. Wings ruffled, stronger scarlet, paler and rosier below. Better shaped than 'Nancy Colledge'. Vigorous, good in the garden as it does not fade, also good for cutting and exhibition. Altogether excellent. Named for the outspoken former manager of Nottingham Forest and Derby County football clubs. Slightly scented. (Unwins, 1982)

'Bridget' (Spencer)
Velvety dark violet-blue. Rather late. Well scented. (Richardson/Unwins, 1996)

'Bright & Breezy' (Spencer)
Mix of six bright clear colours. Well scented.

'Brilliant Fragrance' (Spencer)
Flowers change from cream to soft pink as they develop. Strongly scented.

'Bristol' (Spencer) 🏆 1999
More or less uniform soft blue. Standards upright, open more or less flat with a cream rim then becoming strongly waved; soft blue, slightly paler at the edges; reverse slightly darker. Wings soft blue but slightly darker at the centre; reverse paler. Relatively short but prolific, excellent in the garden and a fine exhibition variety. Strongly scented. (Kerton, 1999)

'Bristol Cream' (Spencer)
Cream. Well scented. (King)

'Buccaneer' (Spencer)
Prolific deep crimson. (King)

'Burnished Bronze' (Spencer)
Glistening maroon, almost brown. Standards shimmering scarlet maroon, slightly waved; reverse the same. Wings waved, some folded down around the keel, slightly less brown; reverse same. Rarely bleaches in strong sun. Similar to 'Karen Reeve', but easier to grow well. Hardly scented.

'Busby' (Original)
Rarely seen pink and white bicolour. Standards slightly muddy rose, white at the base; reverse more peachy. Wings white, veined rose; reverse more or less white. Keel white. The whole flower opens strongly coloured, then fades. Also sometimes known as 'The Busby Pea'. (1823)

'Butterfly' (Original)
"Standard mauve shaded on white, wings white, tinged with lavender. The rim of both wings and standard is dark blue. Medium size, hooded form, the standard notched on the sides. Is one of the oldest varieties of the hooded form." (LM) Suttons themselves described it as "pure white, edged with lavender blue; distinct and beautiful". Strongly scented. (Suttons, 1878)

'Butter Ice' (Modern Grandiflora)
Soft cream. Strongly scented.

'Cambridge Blue' (Spencer)
Very pale silvery blue. Standards upright, well waved, silver white, tinted very pale blue, slightly darker in the centre; reverse the same. Wings well ruffled, same colour, uniform; paler and silvered below. Up to five large blooms per stem. Strongly scented. (Unwins, 1988) There was also a 'Cambridge Blue' (Holmes, 1914) and a 'Cambridge' (Colledge) awarded an HC in 1963.

'Camilla' (Spencer)
Long-stemmed, well-frilled, soft lavender flowers on white. Well scented. (Unwins, 1992)

'Can-Can' (Spencer)
Soft pink, shading to white at the base, generally duplex. Well scented. (Unwins, 1987)

'Candy' (Spencer)

Handsomely patterned chocolate maroon stripe. Standards silvered ivory on the front with maroon wire and a speckled zone at the base; reverse almost completely maroon – a solid picotee edge, then to a speckled zone, then to a more or less solid maroon zone, then silvery around the calyx. Wings a reverse of standards, with an especially solid stripe above the keel; reverse pewter. Keel slightly creamy silver, purple shading on the top. Late flowering, with flowers a little smaller than many modern stripes. A very pretty garden variety, and for cutting. Well scented. There was an earlier 'Candy' (Cullen), a bright pink on white, awarded an AM in 1953.

'Candy Frills' (Spencer)

Vigorous silvery lavender pink, overlaid with silver lilac. Well scented. (Bolton)

'Candyman' (Spencer)

Mixture of striped types. (Fothergill)

'Captain of the Blues' (Grandiflora)

"Standard almost clear purple, wings blue, shaded and tinged with purple. It changes soon after being fully expanded to standard bluish-purple, wings clear blue." (LM) Well scented. (Eckford, 1889) There was also a 'Captain of the Blues Spencer' (Morse, 1909), described as "a very good Spencer form of this variety". (RS)

'Captain Scott' (Spencer)

Frilly, long-stemmed white. Well scented. (Bolton)

'Cara Hepworth' (Spencer)

Very large, bright and bold shimmering pink. Standards broad, well ruffled, sometimes leaning forwards, carmine rose, darker in the centre, silvery white showing through; reverse much the same. Wings darker, tightly ruffled, sometimes slightly folded down over the keel, carmine rose, almost scarlet above, pale at the edge; paler below. All becoming more red with age. Keel white, edged carmine. Some duplex flowers and an occasional distorted flower. Well scented. (Walker, 2001)

'Carlotta' (Spencer)

Deep rich carmine.

'Castle of Mey' (Spencer)

An elegant and classic soft cream. Buds a rather attractive primrose cream, opening to pearly white with cream edges then quickly developing to a full cream. Standard soft cream, darker in the centre, well ruffled, folded back in the oldest flowers; reverse slightly darker and creamier but not always visible. Ruffled wings folded round the keel, spreading later, with faint pink veining towards the base. Keel cream. Very frilly when grown well. Named for the private home of Queen Elizabeth, the Queen Mother. Well scented. (Unwins, 2001)

'Catherine' (Spencer)

Rose pink, with salmony tints, with a white centre. Vigorous. Well scented. (Unwins, 1985)

'Cathy' (Modern Grandiflora)

Very simple and elegant cream Grandiflora with relatively large flowers. Standards upright, rounded and flat; very uniform cream; reverse slightly darker. Wings very uniform cream, angled down over the keel, slightly darker than standards; lip rolled down; reverse slightly paler. Strongly scented. Very pretty, lovely. (Unwins, 2002)

'Cathy Wright' (Spencer)

Pure white. Well scented. (Eagle)

'CCC' (Modern Grandiflora)

White. (Grayson, 1998)

'Champagne Bubbles' (Spencer)

Unique and very pretty well ruffled salmon and cream. Standards rosy salmon on a cream ground; cream at the edge then salmon towards the base; reverse very slightly darker. Wings cream, hazing to pale salmon towards the edges. The colour deepens after cutting. Strongly scented. (Unwins, 1986)

'Charles Unwin' (Spencer)

A very pretty soft shade and closer to a true salmon than most. Standard upright, broadly

A   'Mrs Collier'
B   'Lord Nelson'
C   'Painted Lady'
D   'Lady Grisel Hamilton'
E   'Nellie Viner'
F   'Cupani'

waved; soft salmon pink, paling to salmon-tinted cream at the lobes; slightly softer on the reverse. Wings as standards, often fading less at the edges. Cream keel. Lovely. Vigorous and effective in the garden. Strongly scented. (Colledge) There was also a hooded cream Grandiflora named 'Charles Unwin' (Unwins, 1907) and described by Robert Sydenham as "poor".

'Charlie' (Spencer)
The earliest dark purple. Buds colour early, but the effect is slightly messy-looking. Standards blackish-purple, duskier on the reverse, shinier on the front. Wings less black and more purple. Exceptionally dark, but the whole flower becomes brownish with age. (Unwins, 2002)

'Charlie's Angel' (Spencer) 🏆 1993
Exceptionally delightful pure pale blue. Standards short, almost hooded then rolled back; pale silvery blue, darkening slightly and becoming lavender-tinted with age; some more or less flat, some with a slight wave, some more ruffled. Wings as standards, ruffling again varies slightly; tend to fold down. Large flowers, good in the garden, for cutting and for exhibition, with long stems even when grown on a bush. One of the best. Tends to bunch its flowers for some exhibitors. Strongly scented. (Hanmer)

'Charlotte Ryley' (Modern Grandiflora)
Violet. (Grayson, 1997)

'Chatsworth' (Spencer)
Well-frilled flowers of pale lavender blue, tending to produce five or even six flowers per stem. Well scented.

'Cheri Amour' (Spencer)
Bicolour blend of pink, rose and soft lavender.

'Cherry Ice' (Modern Grandiflora)
Rather different from others in the Ice Series. Small flowers, often only one or two per stem. Standards slightly ruffled, darker than 'Raspberry Ice', with some magenta at the base in some flowers. Wings folded down and rolled. Good colour but few flowers and small. Strongly scented.

'Cheshire Blue' (Grandiflora)
Unusually deep blue. Strongly scented.

'Chocolate Flake' (Spencer)
Mahogany stripes on an off-white background.

'Claire Elizabeth' (Spencer)
Prolific picotee, delicate rose pink edging to the white flower. Well scented. (Hunt)

'Colin Unwin' (Spencer) 🏆 1994
Sun-proof scarlet rose. In the same colour range as 'Brian Clough' and 'Nancy Colledge'. Standards rounded, slightly ruffled, pale scarlet rose, paler at the edges all round; slightly less orange on the reverse. Wings slightly waved, watery scarlet, paler at lobes, and paler below. Well scented. (Colledge)

'Colorcade' (Spencer)
An Australian mixture of highly fragrant Spencer types. Strongly scented.

'Columbus' (Spencer)
Clear light blue Semi-multiflora (paler than 'Cambridge Blue') with long stems, each usually carrying at least five, and often more, well-ruffled flowers on long stems. Well scented. (Unwins, 1993)

'Comet' (Spencer)
Buds yellowish-cream, flushed in red. Flowers of medium size, with a white ground colour and cerise striping on both sides; markings are darker on the back of the standards and top of wings; there is also a cerise wire on back of standards and top of wings. (Unwins, 1998)

'Concorde' (Spencer)
Bright carmine rose. Strongly scented. (King)

Constellation Series (Intermediate)
An alternative name for the New Century Series (page 75).

'Continental' (Spencer)
Mix of many well-ruffled flowers and some

'Columbus'

Grandiflora types in maroon, dark blue, white, pale blue, scarlet, sugar pink and mauve.

'Continental' (Intermediate)
An improved Jet-Set type, with tendrils, in seven colours on plants reaching about 90cm/3ft in height. Up to seven flowers per stem in scarlet, crimson, rose crimson, mid blue, light blue, lavender and white.

'Corinne' (Spencer)
Well-waved carmine rose shading to white at the base. Well scented. (Bolton)

'Countess Cadogan' (Grandiflora)
"Standard opens nearly purple but changes to lilac and later to blue, wings bright blue, shading lighter at the edges. Whole effect quite a bright blue in well matured flowers. 'Captain of the Blues' is a dark 'Countess Cadogan'." (LM) "Rich violet blue standard with a slight flush of mauve at the back; lighter wings...; usually has three flowers on a stem; a useful and very desirable variety for all large collections." (RS) (Eckford, 1889)

'Countess Spencer' (Spencer)
"The original Spencer type Sweet Pea and to the present day one of the best pinks. The colour is bright clear pink on a white ground. The pink deepens towards the edge of the standard. Standard and wings beautifully waved. Strong grower and bears numerous fours." (LM) (page 9) (Cole, 1904)

'Cream Beauty' (Spencer)
Deep cream with especially strongly waved standards. Strongly scented. (B. R. Jones)

'Cream Delight' (Spencer)
Large-flowered rich cream.

'Creameona' (Spencer)
Pretty, small-flowered cream. A definite cream at first but fades to white, hence almost more white than cream. Standards upright, prettily waved, rolled back at the base and creased down the centre; uniform cream colour. Wings nicely rippled, downward sloping around the keel, very slightly paler than standards. Keel clearly visible, also cream with a darker tip.

'Cream Ripple' (Spencer)
Cream, striped with purple.

'Cream Southbourne' (Spencer)
A genuine cream, slightly late. Standards upright, prettily waved; uniform cream, although slightly darker towards the edge, with a hint of amber; slightly more yellow on the reverse. Wings messy and uneven, held almost vertically around the keel which is revealed between, when grown as a bush; very well formed when grown well on a cordon; slightly paler than standards. Strongly scented. (Colledge, 1982)

'Cream Triumph' (Spencer)
Creamy white, only slightly frilled. Well scented. (A. Woodcock)

'Cupani' (Original)
The original sweet pea. Standard vivid deep maroon, peaked at the top and angled forward, white at the base; reverse the same. Wings mauve,

angled down and folded around the keel; pale silvery lavender below. Keel white, and purple along the base. Sometimes includes white rogues or purple/wine bicolours. The fact that most stocks boast three or four flowers per stem seems unlikely to be the result solely of generous cultivation and is probably due to more recent selection. Strongly scented. See 'Original'.

'Cupid' (Dwarf)

White. The original 'Cupid'. A mutation with dramatically shortened internodes creating a very dwarf plant. Found as a sport of 'Emily Henderson', one of the finest white Grandifloras of its day. "The stems are quite procumbent, stout and with numerous short joints from which the flowers are produced; these are about the size of an ordinary Sweet Pea and pure white. The importance of this remarkable break cannot be overestimated... ." *The Garden*, July 4, 1896. (Burpee, 1895) (page 27)

'Cupid Mixed' (Dwarf)

Mix of all, or some, colours in the Cupid Series.

'Cupid Pink' (Dwarf) 🏆 1995

The best of the Cupid Series, a prolific pink and white bicolour.

Cupid Series (Dwarf)

The modern series includes the following 11 colours: Pink, Carmine Bicolour, Deep Lilac, Scarlet Bicolour, White Bicolour, White, Rose, Crimson, Cherry, Salmon Rose, Lavender. (Floranova, 2000)

'Curbar Edge' (Spencer)

Deep rose pink. Hardly scented. (Albutt)

Cuthbertsons

An early-flowering series, rarely grown in the UK, more popular in the US (page 35). 'Danny' – dark blue; 'Evelyn' – salmon rose; 'Frank' – lavender; 'Janet' – white; 'Jimmy' – scarlet; 'Kenneth' – crimson; 'Lois' – rose pink.

A	*'Apricot Sprite'*
B	*'Dragonfly'*
C	*'Apricot Sprite'*
D	*'Larkspur'*

An engraving of the original award-winning display of 'Cupid' sweet peas in 1895.

'Daily Mail' (Spencer)
Very pretty, uniform bold cerise pink. Strong cerise pink, uniform colour over standards and wings. Standards neatly rippled, even cerise pink, creamy white at base. Wings as standards, broadly ruffled, but with a darker zone along ridge over keel. Keel white, wired in the same shade. Well scented. (Beane)

'Dalemain' (Spencer)
Large-flowered ruby red.

'Dave Thomas'

'Dancing Queen' (Spencer)
Classically ruffled in pure white. Standards open white, tinged slightly with green, then develop to pure white with no hint of pink; strongly ruffled, and folded back to a greater or lesser extent. Wings broad, pure white, with the tiniest hint of pink, broadly ruffled. Both standards and wings are the same colour both sides. Strongly scented. (Bolton)

'Daphne' (Spencer)
Long-stemmed, pale lavender. Standards slightly ruffled; pale lavender, slightly darker in the centre; reverse darker, cream at the top at first. Wings more ruffled; slightly darker, paler at the edges, reverse paler. More even in colour than 'Isabella Cochrane'. Strongly scented. (Unwins, 1993)

'Darcey Bussell' (Spencer)
Pretty and elegant pale, rosy purple stripe. Buds rich creamy yellow, eventually purple shortly before opening. Standards narrowly waved, almost crimped; white, with a slight murkiness from the colour on the back; hint of purple wire and a purple vertical mark up the centre, varying from a streak to a fan-shaped zone; reverse purple with almost no white zone between the purple colouring and the purple wire. Wings waved, not rolled under, sometimes rather uneven and unbalanced with noticeable split in the centre; well wired and "striped" with little gap between. Well scented. Named for the Royal Ballet's Principal Ballerina. (Unwins, 2001)

'Dave Thomas' (Spencer) 🏆 1997
Bright, but sometimes slightly watery scarlet. Standards open relatively flat, then ruffled, uniform scarlet colour though paling a little at the edges; reverse slightly paler. Wings same as standards, paler below with white marks either side of the keel. Keel tip partially orange scarlet, rest white. Strongly scented. (Harrod)

'David Unwin' (Spencer)
Large, broadly ruffled pale vermilion. Standards open rounded and unruffled then develop tight waves in very uniform soft pale vermilion, paler at the edges; reverse shimmery. Wings

A   'Anniversary'
B   'Lizbeth'
C   'Champagne Bubbles'
D   'Princess Juliana'
E   'Southbourne'
F   'Frolic'
G   'Tell Tale'

broadly ruffled, same colour as standards, paler below. Rather late, but with long stems. (Unwins, 2002)

'Daphne' growing on hazel brushwood supports in a mixed border.

'Dawn' (Spencer)
Pale lavender blue. Standards hazed lavender blue with white at the edge, strongly reflexed. Wings rippled, same colour as standards and the same below. Keel white, yellow at the tip. Altogether soft and silvery. Vigorous. Strongly scented. (Beane) There was also a 'Dawn' Grandiflora: "A small white, flushed with pale rose at the back of the standard. Three flowers on a stem, but they are too small to be worth attention." (RS) But "Standard light crimson magenta, wings white shaded crimson." (GWK)! (Stark, c. 1906)

'Dawn Chorus' (Intermediate) 🏆 1997
Small Spencer-style flowers on a vigorous Intermediate plant. Standards waved, white with purple on the reverse; wings spreading, also waved, same colour. Slight scent. (Place)

'Dean's Scarlet' (Spencer)
Scarlet, overlaid with orange. Does not fade in the sun.

'D.E.B.R.A' (Spencer)
Mauve.

'Delicacy' (Spencer)
Long-stemmed palest pink. Well scented.

'Denis Compton' (Spencer)
Large-flowered frilly soft pink, pale cream at the centre. Strongly scented. (Bolton)

'Denise Tanner' (Modern Grandiflora)
Standards and wings peachy pink. Hooded standards, red peduncles. Strongly scented. (Grayson)

'Destiny' (Spencer)
Pale pink on a white ground. Hardly scented.

'Diamond Wedding' (Spencer)
Pure white flowers on vigorous plants; often five or six flowers on long stems. Strongly scented. (Unwins, 1980)

'Diana' (Spencer)
Standards slightly ruffled, soft orange salmon, paler at the edges, cream edge on reverse. Wings slightly more orange, paler below, white at the edges. Some duplex flowers. Good in both scorching and wet weather. Hardly scented. (Unwins, 1985)

'Dignity' (Spencer)
Deep royal purple on long stems. (F. Woodcock)

'Dolly Varden' (Grandiflora)
Contemporary opinions differ: "Lavender, shaded to white; good standard; rather lighter wings; medium size...; generally three flowers on a stem." (RS) "Standard bright purple magenta, shading lighter, almost white on the sides and pencilled with heavy maroon at the base." (GWK) Named for the character in Charles Dickens's Barnaby Rudge, the Alaskan migratory trout or, perhaps, the hat. (Burpee, 1898)

'Donna Jones' (Modern Grandiflora)
Bright red. Strongly scented. (Grayson, 1997)

'Dorothy Eckford' (Grandiflora) ♆ 1997
Lovely distinctive pure white. Standards pure white, shaped like the prow of a ship, sides angled back and the top leaning forward; reverse slightly creamy.

Wings broad, partly angled down, slightly folded forward; pure white, front and back. Very pretty and useful in the garden. Usually three flowers per stem. "A very strong grower and a very free bloomer;... the best white." (RS) "Is semi-hooded of the best form with large wings and very large standard which averages two inches across." (LM) Named for Henry Eckford's granddaughter. Strongly scented. (Eckford, 1901)

'Dragonfly' (Semi-Grandiflora)
Cream flecked with light blue. (1930s)

'Duchess of Roxburghe' (Spencer)
Pale blue with a hint of cream. Well scented. (Unwins, 1984)

'Duke of York' (Grandiflora)
An exquisite bicolour. Standards vertical, more or less flat, pale rose, fading to peachy white at the edge and white at the base; reverse similar but peachier. Wings pure white, angled over keel, slightly rolled under. Keel white. Lovely. "Bright carmine rose standard; paler wings; rather more carmine than 'Blanche Ferry'. The standard reflexes very much; a very indifferent flower at times and not wanted." (RS) (Eckford, 1895)

'Dusty Springfield' (Spencer)
Large-flowered scarlet rose. Large, upright standards, scarlet rose, crimped in the centre, flat at the sides, generally rounded in shape; slightly darker on the reverse. Wings darker, sometimes almost scarlet becoming less so with age, slightly paler below, white at the base. (Unwins, 2002)

'Dynasty' (Spencer)
Very striking carmine. Standards upright, slightly waved, dense carmine veining on white, more uniform colour on the reverse. Wings denser in colour, hardly waved, hanging down at the sides, paler below. Vigorous. Well scented. (Unwins, 1986)

'Earl Spencer' (Spencer)
"This is a grand new variety. May best be described as a large and beautiful orange, or salmon-orange self of the Spencer type...; I am afraid it will prove very

disappointing unless grown in the shade, and cut in bud state and opened in water." RS (Cole, 1908)

Early Multiflora Gigantea
Page 35. Varieties in this series include: 'Chloe' – navy blue; 'Eleanor' – mid blue; 'Flag Blue' – navy blue; 'Gloria' – deep rose-pink; 'Grace' – lavender; 'Lily' – white; 'Marilyn' – scarlet cerise; 'Peaches' – salmon on cream; 'Stella' – cream; 'Susie' – light salmon pink.

'Early Sunshine' (Spencer)
Australian mixture of Spencer types.

'Eckford's Mix' (Grandiflora)
Mixture of varieties raised by Henry Eckford. Strongly scented.

'Eclipse' (Spencer)
Large-flowered purple with a very ruffled look. Standards strongly waved, reflexed, very striking cerise purple and very even, slightly paler at the edges; reverse same. Wings strongly ruffled, slightly darker than standards, slightly paler below and slightly silvered. Keel white, edged purple. Very reliable. Strongly scented. (Unwins, 1975)

'Ed Fincham' (Spencer)
Nicely waved maroon. Slightly scented. (Harrod)

'Edward Unwin' (Spencer)
Prolific and large-flowered clear blue. Larger-flowered than 'Charlie's Angel'. Strongly scented. (Unwin, 1994)

'Eileen Brinton' (Spencer)
Soft pearly rose. Standards open cream, slightly flushed with pink, then become more white and more strongly coloured as they mature; eventually rose pink and slightly creamy white at the base and the lobes; well ruffled; reverse paler. Wings often open more strongly flushed pink than the standards, with creamy white edges, paler below, generally well ruffled. Keel cream. Sometimes with strongly reddish rogues which ruins the effect. (Albutt, 2001)

'Elaine Paige' (Spencer)
Bright rose pink. Named for the singer.

'Elegance' (Spencer)
Pure white. There was also a Grandiflora 'Elegance': "A very pretty bright rose flaked or veined variety, upright standard, generally two, sometimes three, flowers on a stem; the colour on the standard and wings is different at times." (RS) (Stark, 1908)

'Elinor' ♔ 1996
Closely spaced flowers in white, flushed with reddish purple, with waved standards and rather hooded, waved wings. Strongly scented. (D. M. Jones)

'Elizabeth Taylor' (Spencer)
Large-flowered clear mauve with very frilly flowers. Unusually heat-tolerant. Well scented. Named for the film star when she was just 19. (Unwins, 1951)

'Ella' (Spencer)
Carmine ruby.

'Emma' (Spencer)
Pretty pale salmon rose. Standards gently ruffled, opening cream with a touch of pink, quickly becoming more strongly flushed with salmon rose though creamier at the lobes and slightly cream in the centre; reverse paler. Wings gently waved, slightly darker, more completely blushed with colour, slightly silvered below.

'Ena Margaret' (Spencer)
Purple picotee. Strongly scented. (Everitt)

'England's Queen' (Modern Grandiflora)
White, with double notched standards. Four flowers per stem. Identical to Eckford's 'Queen of England'. Strongly scented. (Grayson, 1997)

'Enid Walker' (Spencer)
Long-stemmed and well-balanced pale blue. Strongly scented.

'Esther Rantzen' (Spencer)
Lavender blue. Named for the TV personality.

'Ethel Grace' (Spencer)
Lavender, vigorous and long-stemmed. Well scented. (BR Jones)

'Eva Bridger' (Spencer)
Mauve pink. Strongly scented.

'Evening Glow' (Spencer) ♈ 1996
A non-gardener's idea of a sweet pea. Standards not ruffled when first open, edges rolled slightly forward then gently ruffled; cream at the base, quickly hazing to coral orange, creamier on the reverse. Wings hardly waved at first then strongly ruffled, or almost fluted; slightly darker than the standards, paler below, with a large white zone at the base. Keel cream, with a slightly yellow tip. Very pretty, with a very rounded Grandiflora look when young. Well scented. (Beane)

'Evensong' (Spencer)
Soft bluish-lilac. Strongly scented. (Unwins, 1960)

'Explorer Mixed' ♈ 1994
Mixture of the colours below. Well scented. (Bodger)

Explorer Series (Intermediate)
Impressive successor to 'Snoopea' and 'Supersnoop', this award-winning series is tendril-free with large, sometimes strongly scented flowers carried three or four on a stem – and when well grown, the stems are long enough to cut. Colours: Crimson, Mid Blue, Rose Pink, Scarlet, White, Purple, Navy Blue, Light Pink. (Bodger)

'Fairy Queen' (Original)
"Flesh colour, slightly tinged at times with pink; poor shape, small, stem rather short; of no merit." (RS) (Haage and Schmidt, 1874)

'Fandango' (Spencer)
Comprehensive mixture of flake varieties for garden and cutting. Slightly scented. (Unwins, 2001) There is also a mauve Spencer of this name (Gubb) which received an AM in 1991.

'Fanny Adams' (Spencer)
Magenta. Well scented. (Grayson, 1997)

'Fantasia' (Dwarf)
Fragrant mixture including shades of purple, mauve, pink, rose, light blue, red and white, as well as some bicolours and a few more unusual shades. Useful for baskets, window boxes and the front of the border.

'Fatima' (Spencer)
Rich glowing scarlet, slightly silvered. Slightly scented. (Unwins, 1989)

'Felicity Kendal' (Spencer)
Large and vigorous rich cerise pink. Named for the actress. Strongly scented.

'Fiona' (Spencer)
Large frilly, often duplex, flowers in salmon pink fading to cream at the centre. Often with five or more flowers per stem. Strongly scented. (Unwins, 1980)

'Firebird' (Spencer)
Orange-red. Hardly scented. (Albutt)

'Firecrest' (Spencer)
Rich sun-proof orange scarlet. Well scented. (Bolton)

'First Lady' (Spencer)
Cream with a carmine flush. Does not fade. Strongly scented. (King)

'Flakes Mixed' (Spencer)
Mixture of flake types including sugar pink, carmine, magenta, purple, rose, bright scarlet.

'Flamenco' (Spencer)
Small flowers, only slightly ruffled. Standards orange on the front, reverse paler. Wings softer orange, paling at the edges, paler below. Keel pale orange. Rather weak in growth.

'Flora Cave' (Spencer)
Flowers closely spaced, white, flushed with red, the standards reflexed and waved with the wings spreading and waved. Slightly scented. (Cave)

'Floral Tribute' (Spencer)
Mixture of Spencer types chosen for both exhibition and garden performance. Well scented.

'Flora Norton' (Grandiflora) ♗ 1995
"A pale blue... has a beautiful upright standard, but small and rather too large wings in proportion to the standard. A very desirable variety, used rarely to have more than two flowers on a stem, but now often has three." (RS) (Morse, 1905). Strongly scented. There was also a 'Flora Norton Spencer' (Morse, 1908), "generally with four flowers on a stem". (RS)

'Florence' (Spencer)
Widely spaced white flowers, flushed with red, paler at the edge. Well waved. Slightly scented. (Beane) There was also an earlier 'Florence' (House, 1908) "Too near 'Marjorie Wallis' ". (RS) 'Marjorie Wallis' was a bright rose pink form of 'Countess Spencer'.

'Florencecourt' (Spencer) ♗ 1999
Large, well-formed salmon cerise. Standards reflexed, waved, white heavily flushed in salmon cerise; wings waved, spreading same colour as standards. Slight scent. (Harrod)

'Floriada' (Dwarf)
Bright dwarf carmine. Standards slightly ruffled, top folded forward, almost scarlet. Wings ruffled, folded down, paler below with a white mark at the base.

'Flower Arrangers' Blend' (Spencer)
Strong-growing blend of pastels, picotees and stripes producing long, straight stems. (Unwins)

'Fragrantissima' (Spencer)
A mixture of award-winning varieties with the emphasis on a strong fragrance. Strongly scented.

'Fragrant Ripples' (Spencer)
Mix of stripes in scarlet, claret, blue and lilac. Well scented.

'Frances Perry' (Spencer)
Well-frilled flowers of salmon pink. Vigorous and sun-proof. Named for the distinguished garden writer. Slightly scented. (Unwins, 1981)

'Frolic' (Spencer)
Very pretty rose picotee on strong cream. Standards slightly ruffled, opening cream, becoming increasingly pink-veined and slightly more ruffled; reverse is generally less pink and more pearly. Wings almost entirely cream, clasped around the keel, opening out and becoming more strongly pink-veined with age but remaining more or less cream below. Keel cream. Some duplex flowers. Varies slightly in the degree of pink veining. Strongly scented. (Burpee)

'Full Stop' (Spencer)
Very pretty blend of stripes in maroon, dark and light blue, cerise and purple plus self colours in white, blue and sugar pink to create a blend of stripes and plain colours which harmonize well. (Unwins)

'Gaiety' (Spencer)
Like a Spencer 'Painted Lady'. Bright pink standards and white wings. Slightly scented. There was also a 'Gaiety' Grandiflora: "A nice flower, flaked or striped with rosy magenta; generally has three flowers on a stem, and one of the best and brightest of the striped section." (RS) (Eckford, 1893)

Galaxy Series
An exceptionally vigorous and prolific strain, starting to bloom earlier and continuing for longer than the Spencer type. Long, strong stems produce five to seven flowers, usually well scented. The colours are shades of: Blue, Pink, Scarlet, Cerise, Cream, Rose, and White. Usually only a mixture is available.

'Garden News' (Spencer)
Unusually fragrant bright scarlet. Standards broadly waved, misty pale scarlet, edged white, fading increasingly orange-scarlet. Wings as standards but paler below; overall a slightly messy look. Well scented.

'Geniana' (Dwarf/Intermediate) ♗ 2000
Pretty, long-flowering violet picotee. Reaching 60cm/24in, with two or three flowers on short stems, this is an early- and long-flowering variety. Standards and the spreading wings of the small,

'Glow'

slightly waved flowers are white with a violet picotee edge. Strongly scented. (Levko)

'Geoff Amos' (Spencer)
Large-flowered, deep crimson stripe. Named for the veteran garden writer. Well scented.

'Geoff Hamilton' (Spencer)
Large deep purple. Named for the much-loved TV gardener. Well scented.

'Geranium Pink' (Spencer)
Salmon pink.

'Gertrude Tingay' (Spencer)
Deep lavender. (Bolton)

'Giant Exhibition Mixed' (Spencer)
Wide range of colours, "each spike supporting five or six blooms"!

'Giant Hybrids Mix' (Spencer)
A mixture of Spencer types.

'Giant Waved Mix' (Spencer)
A mixture of Spencer types.

'Glow' (Spencer)
Unique combination of peach and pink. Large elegant flowers, standards peachy, slightly orange pink, broadly waved; wings bright cerise pink. A gorgeous bi-colour. Well scented. (Unwins,1997)

'Gorleston' (Spencer)
Clean bright but deep mauve.

'Grace of Monaco' (Spencer)
Vigorous rosy lavender. Named for the actress Grace Kelly. Well scented. (Williams)

'Gracious Lady' (Spencer)
Long-stemmed pale salmon pink. Well scented.

'Gwendoline', grown on galvanized wire pig netting, which provides stout support.

'Grandiflora Scented' (Grandiflora)
Mixed of highly scented Grandifloras.

'Grayson's Hybrids' (Spencer)
Unfixed hybrid seed. (Grayson)

'Grayson's Mixture' (Spencer)
A mixture of Peter Grayson's Spencer types. (Grayson)

'Great Expectations' (Spencer)
Long-stemmed blend of lilac and lavender shades. Strongly scented.

'Gwendoline' (Spencer) ♛ 1998
Large-flowered, and very dramatic rose and white. Standards upright and well waved, slightly cerisey rose pink, white at the base, paler on reverse. Wings neatly peaked, slightly more waved than standards, fading to white at centre. Strongly scented. (Unwins, 1999) There was an earlier Spencer of the same name, "A good blue of the Spencer type, like 'Flora Norton Spencer', but a richer colour." (RS) (House, 1908)

'Gypsy Queen' (Spencer)
Deep ruby red.

'Gypsy Rose' (Spencer)
Long stems carry up to eight deep but bright rose pink flowers, many duplex. Tough and easy to grow. Slightly scented. (Unwins, 1984)

'Hampton Court' (Spencer)
Prolific and vigorous blue, slightly darker than 'Blue Danube'.

'Hanslope Gem' (Spencer)
Deep carmine pink.

'Hard Times' (Spencer)
Mid blue. Well scented. (Bailey)

'Harvest Time' (Spencer)
Pink-tinted carmine.

'Hazel Tasker' (Spencer)
White, flushed with pink.

'Heartbeat' (Spencer)
Large-flowered bright scarlet-cerise. Standards well ruffled, usually folded back at the sides, opening rose pink and quickly becoming cerise flushed in scarlet, slightly richer colour towards the edge; reverse same. Wings well ruffled, similar in colour though slightly less scarlet, paler below and white towards the base; wings tend to part over the keel. Keel flushed red, white at the base. Well scented. (2001)

'Heathcliff' (Modern Grandiflora)
Large-flowered blue Grandiflora. Initially opening deep blue black. Standards then become upright, rounded, slightly waved, with slightly purplish-blue veins on white; reverse purple blue; some not waved. Wings slightly waved, same colour as standards, paler below. (Unwins, 2002)

'Heirloom Collection' (Grandiflora)
Collection of separately packeted Grandiflora varieties.

'Helen' (Spencer)
Rose pink. Hardly scented. (Truslove)

'Henry Eckford' (Grandiflora)
"It may be said to be the nearest approach to an orange or salmon-orange self variety yet raised; the flowers are rather small and rarely more than two on a stem; unfortunately it scalds very badly in the sun." (RS) Most stocks are modern "improvements". (Eckford, 1904)

'Herald' (Spencer)
Large well-placed salmon rose flowers on long stems.

'Heritage Mixed' (Modern Grandiflora)
A mixture of modern Grandifloras raised by Peter Grayson and chosen from: 'Benjamin Townsend', 'CCC', 'Charlotte Ryley', 'Donna Jones', 'England's Queen', 'Philip Miller' and 'Tovah Martin'. (Grayson)

'Her Majesty' (Spencer)
Bright carmine red. Standards carmine, slightly darker than 'Robert Uvedale', coloured right to the base of the lobe, same on reverse. Wings slightly darker, paler on reverse, almost scarlet at the edges; floppy and slightly rolled. Very tall and with striking red stains at the leaf joints. Well scented. (Unwins, 1993) There was also a Grandiflora of this name: "A rich crimson self; generally two or three flowers on a stem." (RS) (Eckford, 1893). There was also 'Her Majesty Spencer'.

'Hillbury' (Spencer)
Long-stemmed deep crimson.

'Holymoorside' (Spencer)
Cream. Strongly scented. (Entwistle, 1997)

'Honeymoon' (Spencer)
Opens white then develops to a lovely pale lavender blue flush. Excellent for exhibition. Exceptional scent.

'Honeypink' (Spencer)
Standards cerisey pink to white at the base, clumsily waved; sometimes elegantly pointed at the centre. Wings are the same colour, but uneven. Overall appearance slightly messy. Well scented. (Kershaw)

'Horizon' (Spencer)
Extraordinarily comprehensive mixture of colours, including selfs, bicolours and stripes, specially selected for flowering for a long period. Strongly scented. (Hammett)

A few of the colours in 'Horizon Mixed' growing up a rustic garden feature.

'Hunter's Moon' (Spencer)
Large, frilly flowers in rich cream with an almost lemony hint. Strongly scented. (Unwins, 1968)

'Ice Blue'
See 'Blue Ice' (page 46).

Ice Series (Modern Grandifloras)
A series of modern Grandifloras introduced by E. W. King in Britain. The colours are: 'Butter Ice', 'Cherry Ice', 'Raspberry Ice', 'Strawberry Ice' and 'Vanilla Ice'.

'Imogen' (Spencer)
Bold slightly carmine rose. Standards open carmine rose, slightly flushed with scarlet, well ruffled and tending to fold backwards; white at the base; reverse paler. Wings similar, with a slightly uneven cream centre, evenly hazed to cream at the base below. Keel white. Intense and dramatic though soft rather than crude. (Beane, 2001)

'Indigo King' (Grandiflora)
"Standard violet maroon. Wings violet. Under med-ium size, hooded form. Standard is notched on both sides." (LM) (Eckford, 1885)

'Isabella Cochrane' (Spencer)
Large-flowered pretty pastel lilac. Standards open pearly white with a tint of green, then broadly ruffled, to white delicately hazed in lavender, darker towards the centre; white at the edges and white at the centre with a few dark whiskers; pearly behind. Wings broad, coloured as standards, often with a concentrated band of colour along the central edges of the wings; paler below. Intensity of colour varies slightly from plant to plant. Gorgeous, and slightly richer in colour than 'Arthur Hellyer'. Strongly scented. (Chisholm, 2001)

'Ivory Queen' (Spencer)
Cream. Strongly scented. (Harris)

'Jacqueline O'Brien' (Spencer)
Brilliant orange-cerise. Well scented.

'Janet Scott' (Grandiflora) 🏆 1995
"A clear pale salmon pink; hooded standard, and large broad wings. Darker than 'Prima Donna'...; generally three flowers on a stem" (RS) "The unusual size of the wings with the large, substantial hooded standard, gives the flower an appearance of enormous size." (GWK) Strongly scented. (Morse, 1903)

'Jayne Amanda' (Spencer) 🏆 1994
Large and frilly rose pink shading to white at the base. Strongly scented. (Truslove)

Jet Set Series (Intermediate)
For many years the standard for Intermediates, the large-frilled flowers come in Scarlet, Crimson, Blue

Left: 'Jimmy Young'
Below: 'Jet Set Pink' growing on low brushwood
supports showing the prolific flower production.

Salmon, Pink, Cerise, Mauve and Cream with five to seven per stem. Prolific and colourful but now rarely available and then only in a mixture. Many colours won awards in the 1970s. (Ferry–Morse)

'Jewels of Albion' (Grandiflora)
Special blend of heat-tolerant Grandifloras in soft mauve, deep blue, cream and lavender. Strongly scented.

'Jill Walton' (Spencer)
Pretty pale apricot fading to rose. Standards broadly ruffled, opening apricot on reverse, rose on the front, then to slightly creamy white, hazing to rose pink towards the edge; reverse very slightly darker. Wings open slightly pinker then as standards

but paler; underside more or less white. Availability varies as producing a seed crop can be difficult. Strongly scented. (Gubb)

'Jilly' (Spencer) 🏆 1994
Superb cream for garden and exhibition. Buds yellow. Standards broadly and evenly waved, open creamy white with pewtery sparks, paling to slightly ivory white, cream at base. Wings as standards, nicely peaked in the centre, broadly and evenly waved. Altogether superb. Well scented. (Harris, 1988)

'Jimmy MacBain' (Spencer)
Large and frilly, long-stemmed pale pink on a white ground. Well scented.

'Jimmy Young' (Spencer)
Delightful, tall white Multiflora, great in the garden. Buds creamy yellow. Standards slightly waved, sometimes pointed at the top; pure white, slightly pewtered on the back. Wings neat and slightly waved, pure white, neatly angled occasionally with a hint of pink. Long stems. Named for the crooner-turned-radio presenter. (Unwins, 1998)

'John Ness' (Spencer)
Lavender. Well scented. (Carters)

'Joker' (Spencer)
Large-flowered light purple with maroon overtones.

'Juliana' (Spencer)
Rosy red. Hardly scented. (King)

'Juliet' (Modern Grandiflora)
Delightful cream with a hint of pink. Standards open cream, reverse darker, with a haze of pale pink round the rim; then paler, with a faint pink vertical stripe in the centre; very faintly flushed. Wings open cream, pink haze in the centre and edges rolled down; then paler, with very little pink. Keel cream. Calyx and peduncles red. One of my favourite recent introductions for the garden. (Unwins, 2002) There was an earlier 'Juliet', a strongly scented pink on white Intermediate. (King) and also a much earlier Grandiflora "Pale apricot on lemon ground". (LM) (Deal, 1911)

'Karen Louise' (Spencer)
Pale lavender. Strongly scented. (Kings)

'Karen Reeve' (Spencer)
Very large-flowered, intense deep purple maroon. Standards evenly ruffled, evenly purple maroon in colour; reverse slightly darker, with an electric purple flash at the base. Wings same colour as standards, tends to split over the keel, paler below with a distinct sheen. Keel bright pale purple on white. Hardly scented. (Reeve)

'Karen Tremewan' (Spencer)
Pink. (Tremewan)

'Ken Colledge' (Spencer)
Standards silvery mauve, slightly paler at the edges, slightly ruffled; reverse the same. Wings neatly ruffled and well balanced; darker than standards, rich purple, paler at the edges; paler below. Less vigorous than many, with small to medium-sized flowers. Might benefit from re-selection. Named for distinguished sweet pea breeder. Well scented.

'Juliet'

'King Edward VII' (Grandiflora) 🏆 1995
Standards taller than wide, flat, creased in the centre but sometimes peaked; purple, tinted scarlet; reverse the same. Wings magenta, angled down over the keel and folded; reverse pale silvery purple or redder. A tall and dramatic variety, effectively scarlet from a distance "...generally three flowers on a stem; a very fine variety, and undoubtedly the best of its class". (RS) Strongly scented. (Eckford, 1903) There was also a 'King Edward Spencer'. (Burpee, 1909)

'Kingfisher' (Semi-Grandiflora)
Cream, flecked with dark blue. (1930s)

'King of Mauves' (Spencer)
Bright rich purple.

'King's Bounty' (Spencer)
Rosy carmine. (King)

'King's Bride' (Spencer)
Pink with a creamy base. (King)

'King's Cloak' (Spencer)
Deep velvet blue. (King)

'King's Frill' (Spencer)
Pink picotee. (King)

'King Size Navy Blue' (Spencer)
Large and ruffled deep navy blue. Well scented.

'King's Reach' (Spencer)
Medium blue. (King)

'King's Special' (Spencer)
Mixture formulated with garden performance and fragrance in mind. Strongly scented. (King)

'Kippen Cream' (Spencer)
Large, well-placed cream flowers on long stems. Well scented. (Kerton, 1998)

'Kiri Te Kanawa' (Spencer) 🏆 1997
Almond pink, white at the base. Named for the opera singer (Brackley)

'Lavender Bridesmaid', also known as 'Teresa Maureen'

'Kiwi Bicolours Mix' (Spencer)
Mixture of bicoloured types. Well scented. (Hammett)

'Knee-Hi Mixed' (Intermediate) 🏆 2000
Stocks of this ground-breaking variety have been around for many years but few are good; recent Wisley trials reveal stock produced by Bodgers, an American breeder but not retailer, to be the best. Reaching 90–100cm/36–40in in height, with between six and nine flowers per stem, the colours are cream, reddish-purple shades, pink, deep red, violet and purple. The flowers are about 5cm/2in across, with waved standards, but no scent, or occasionally just a little. Originally 1.5m/5ft high and from Ferry–Morse, and often well-scented, separate colours won awards in the 1960s.

'Kyle the Clown' (Spencer)
Dramatic cerise-scarlet stripe. Standards pearly white with a dusting of cerise speckling and fine, neat, cerise-scarlet wire with an almost unspeckled zone between; reverse dusted all over in speckles, most concentrated towards the centre, and with a slightly broader picotee at the edge. Wings bright white, speckled and wired in cerise with a white zone between; reverse white with a hint of

cerise showing through from the other side. Keel white with a cerise line across the top. The colour changes from bright rosy purple in newly opened flowers, becoming more red as the flowers age. Dramatic but slightly variable, with some flowers much less strongly coloured. Well scented. (2001)

'Lady Diana' (Spencer)
Lavender pink flowers on long sturdy stems. Well scented. (Harriss)

'Lady Fairbairn' (Spencer)
Exceptionally large-flowered, long-stemmed lavender rose. Named for the long-serving President of the NSPS. Well scented. (Unwins, 1983)

'Lady Grisel Hamilton' (Grandiflora)
"This was the very best and largest heliotrope or lavender self until the new 'Mrs Charles Foster' appeared. Usually has three, sometimes four, flowers on a stem. The standard hoods considerably; apart from this it is undoubtedly the best in this class or shade of colour in the old type." (RS) Good in heat. Strongly scented. (Eckford, 1899) There was also a 'Lady Grisel Hamilton Spencer'. (Burpee, 1909)

'Lady Penny' (Spencer)
Elegant deep lavender.

'Lady Susan' (Spencer)
Orange pink. (Albutt)

'Lady Turrall' (Modern Grandiflora)
Magenta standard with lilac wings. Two or three flowers per stem.

'Larkspur' (Spencer)
Exquisite pale blue.

'Laura' (Spencer)
Large crimson flowers on stout stems; vigorous. Slightly scented. (Walker)

'Lavender Bridesmaid' (Dwarf) ♛ 2000
Very pretty, small-flowered, dwarf bicolour. Standards very upright, white with pretty purple

whiskers and purple wire; shaded purple at the top; bolt of deep purple on reverse. Wings neatly peaked, creamy white, purple at the edges, whiter below. Small flowers but prolific, very effective and pretty. Strongly scented. Also known as 'Teresa Maureen'. (Cave, 2001)

'Lavender Flake' (Spencer)
Soft lavender on white flake.

'Lavender Stripe' (Spencer)
Lavender on white stripe.

'Leamington' (Spencer)
Strongly waved deep lavender. Strongly scented. (Colledge)

'Lemonade'
See *L. chloranthus* (page 94).

'Lianne Marie' (Spencer)
Large well-placed magenta flowers on long stems. (Eagle Nursery)

'Lilac Ripple' (Spencer)
See 'Pulsar'.

'Lilac Silk' (Spencer)
Delicate pale lilac, with a hint of pink, on cream. Large-flowered and frilly. Well scented. (Bolton)

'Lilac Time' (Spencer)
The colour of dark wild lilac. (Bolton)

'Lillie Langtry' (Spencer)
Large, well-waved, rich cream. Named for the Victorian actress. Slightly scented.

'Lily Price' (Spencer)
Very large-flowered, well-formed, carmine. Well scented.

'Linda C' (Spencer)
Slightly two-tone lavender blue. Standards broadly waved, lavender blue, folded forward when young, standing more upright as the flowers age;

lavender blue with a narrow pale rim, slightly more blue towards the centre; slightly more pearly and more noticeably veined behind. Wings more blue, tending to clasp the keel when young then flattening out, but well ruffled; reverse paler and slightly veined. Keel silvery white, slightly flushed blue. Relatively late, with unusually long, strong, stout stems, excellent for cutting. Colour varies slightly but this is not off-putting. Well scented. (Chisholm, 2001)

'Little Red Riding Hood' (Modern Grandiflora)
A dramatic bicolour with scarlet standards and white wings. A captivating newcomer. (Hammett)

'Little Sweetheart' (Dwarf)
One of a number of rather variable dwarf, patio mixtures. Prolific and usually with seven colours. Slightly scented.

'Little Red Riding Hood'

'Lively Lassie' (Spencer)
Large-flowered white flushed with lilac. Strongly scented. Introduced in their centenary year by Robert Bolton & Sons. (2001)

'Lizbeth' (Spencer) 🏆 1999
Very large flowers in sugar pink with scarlet highlights. Standards upright, nicely ruffled, white at the base; strong rose pink, white at the very edge; reverse darker. Wings darker than standards above, paler below. Tip of keel tends to peep through. Lasts very well in water. Well scented. (Tremewan)

'Liz Bolton' (Spencer)
Delightful almond pink shading to white at the base. (Bolton)

'Lord Nelson' (Grandiflora)
Blue and mauve bicolour. Standards upright, peaked and slightly waved; angled slightly forward; dusky mauve with blue undertones; reverse deep, almost indigo blue. Wings similar but more blue, reverse paler, angled over keel but only slightly folded. "A fine dark purple blue self... generally three, or often four flowers on a stem." (RS) Strongly scented. Introduced by Burpee (1907) as 'Brilliant Blue', renamed by House.

'Louise' (Spencer)
Deep salmon rose with a creamy white base. Slightly scented.

'Lovejoy' (Spencer)
Vigorous deep maroon. Unusually hard-seeded.

'Lovely Lady' (Spencer)
Very pretty, washed denim blue. Relatively small flowers, each more or less uniform in colour and only slightly ruffled. Standards upright, hazed blue over white with a cream edge, slightly silvered on the reverse. Wings the same. Keel blue on top and point. (Unwin, 2001) There was an earlier 'Lovely Lady', a pink picotee on white, trialled in 1982. (Thomas)

'Love Match' (Spencer)
A mixture of strongly scented bicoloured forms including pale pink on rosy carmine, white on lavender, carmine pink on rose, violet on blue and white on carmine. Also known as 'Romance' and 'Kiwi Bicolours'. Strongly scented. (Hammett)

'Lucinda Jane' (Spencer)
Strawberry pink. Well scented. (Grayson, 1997)

'Lustre' (Spencer)
Rosy carmine. (Unwins, 1979)

'Lymmer' (Dwarf)
Standards flat, rose pink on the front and reverse. Wings white, edges ruffled under, fading to all white. Small flowers.

'Lynn Davey' (Spencer)
Very long-stemmed, large ruffled blue. Standards slightly waved, blue, darker in the centre and paler at the edge; reverse darker. Wings more ruffled and darker than standards; reverse paler. When young, the standards are mauve, cream at the edge, wings blue. Strongly scented. (James)

'Lynn Fiona' (Spencer)
Large, beautifully waved cream flowers with a pink blush. Long stems with exceptional tolerance of bad weather. Strongly scented.

'Macmillan Nurse' (Spencer)
Very pretty soft salmon pink. Opens slightly salmon rose, then to fades to pale rose. Standards upright and broadly ruffled, with a neat rose wire, shading through pale rose to white at the centre; reverse the same. Wings more or less horizontal or angled to a peak over the keel, ruffled, white with pink picotee, less colour than standard. Named for the nursing charity. Well scented. (Unwins, 1996)

'Maggie May' (Spencer)
Elegantly waved, pale sky blue, flushed with white. Strongly scented. (Thomas)

'Magic' (Spencer)
Pink flush on a "lemon" ground.

'Magic Mixed' (Spencer)
Striped mixture. Well scented.

Mammoth Series
Page 35. Colours include Mid Blue, Lavender, White, Salmon Cream Pink, Deep Rose, Scarlet, Crimson.

'Margaret Joyce' (Spencer) 🏆 1997
Well-coloured blue, tolerant of bad weather. Well scented. (Robertson)

'Margot' (Spencer)
Large-flowered cream.

'Marguerite' (Spencer)
Pale lavender blush on white. Well scented.

'Marie's Melody' (Intermediate) 🏆 1996
Lovely bushy stripe. Exceptional shape and pattern, small but not tiny flowers, waved. Standards silvered white with magenta vertical stripe and wire; reverse darkly veined, bold wire. Wings opposite of standards (Place)

'Marion' (Spencer)
Exceptional impact, very bold and impressive lavender. Standards strong silvery lavender, evenly waved, cream at the edge at first; reverse darker. Wings the same, paler at the edge and paler below. Very uniform colour, with the extra benefit of a red-tinted calyx, peduncle and top of stem. Large flowers on long stems. Excellent for exhibition and unusually resistant to bud drop. Strongly scented. There was an earlier 'Marion', a pale lilac rose, introduced in 1911 and another in 1932.

'Marmalade Skies' (Spencer) 🏆 1994
Standards hooded, waved, white heavily streaked, flushed and edged in red; wings hooded, waved, colour as standards. Strongly scented. (Beane)*

'Mars' (Spencer)
Brilliant coloured stripe; exceptional. Buds creamy

green with a red flush and red wire. Standards shaded white on front, wired scarlet, with dense radiation of even speckles on the reverse. Wings white, scarlet blood red on the inner edges, with dense speckling on either side; white underneath. The wings are folded under at the sides and this reduces the impact. Well scented. (Unwins, 1996) There was also a Grandiflora 'Mars': "A large, rich, dark fiery-crimson self...; wings slightly flushed with purple; usually three, sometimes four, flowers on a stem." (RS) "An intense crimson scarlet, and of the largest Grandiflora form. This is the first scarlet that has reached the full size and hooded shape." (WTH) (Eckford, 1897)

'Martha Lane Fox' (Spencer)
Large-flowered prolific deep scarlet with strong stems and good placement. Named for the internet entrepreneur. Well scented. (Brackley, 2001)

'Marti Caine' (Spencer)
Excellent deep scarlet. Standards scarlet with dark veins; reverse the same; strongly reflexed and waved. Wings slightly paler, but strong scarlet around the edges and noticeably veined darker. Keel more or less white, with red streaks. Named for the popular singer. Slightly scented. (Beane)

'Mary Malcolm' (Spencer)
Delicate apricot pink, fades in bright sun.

'Mary Rose' (Spencer)
Large and prolific frilly rose pink flowers shading to white at the base.

'Matucana' (Grandiflora)
Deep maroonish-purple standard, with bluish-mauve wings. Strongly scented. Not, as so often stated, the "original" sweet pea and not from Sicily but found in Peru (page 6). Good in summer heat. Strongly scented.

'Matucana Mix' (Grandiflora)
A misleading name, sometimes bewilderingly used for the single colour (above), sometimes for a mix of Grandifloras.

'Matucana'

'Mauve King' (Spencer)
Deep mauve.

'Maytime' (Spencer)
Vigorous almond pink on white. Well scented.

'Melody' (Spencer)
Mixture of up to six different bicoloured forms: pink on white, orchid on white, rose on pale pink, salmon on pale pink, navy on blue and deep rich maroon on violet. Strongly scented. (Hammett) There was also a Grandiflora 'Melody', "a very pretty soft pink" (RS) (Chapman, 1908); a Spencer 'Melody' (Unwins, 1936) and a Spencer 'Melodie' (Unwins, 1965). Also known as 'Bicolour Melody' and 'Rare Melody'.

'Memorial Flight' (Spencer)
Large and very frilly white with stout stems. Good exhibition variety. Strongly scented.

'Memories' (Spencer)
Warm rose pink on a white ground. Strongly scented.

'Midnight' (Spencer)
Sultry, deep maroon. Standards strongly and evenly waved, very upright, dark chocolate with a bright purple flash at the base and as dark behind. Wings very slightly more purple, paling at the edges with a white flash underneath at the base and a paler keel. Vigorous. Hardly scented. (Unwins, 1986) There was also a Grandiflora 'Midnight', also known as 'Jet': "Standard deep purplish-maroon, almost black; wings claret" (RS) (Burpee, 1908); and an earlier Spencer 'Midnight'. (Unwins, 1957)

'Milestone' (Spencer)
Large, well-shaped, deep maroon, slightly bronzed. Well scented. (Unwins, 1971)

'Millennium' (Spencer) ♔ 1997
Very large ruffled magenta rose. Standards pale magenta, slightly waved, tending to lean forward, paling towards the lobes; very slightly paler on the reverse. Wings elegant though sometimes split, broadly waved, pale magenta blush towards the centre; paler and slightly silvered below. Bright, colourful with good impact. Well scented. (D. M. Jones)

'Millennium Mixed' (Spencer)
A mixture containing all the current varieties listed by Robert Bolton & Sons, together with some still under development. Well scented. (Bolton, 2000)

'Min's Ambition' (Spencer)
Deep rosy mauve. Well scented. (F. Woodcock)

'Minuet' (Intermediate mix)
Bushy striped mix. A very pretty formula blend of scarlet, pale mauve, crimson, blue and rose. (Unwins, 2001)

'Miranda Crafer' (Spencer)
Vigorous carmine with stout stems, rather late. Slightly scented. (Walker)

'Miss Truslove' (Spencer)
Exceptional pale mauve though with more than a hint of pink. Slightly scented.

'Miss Willmott' (Grandiflora)
"Standard orange pink, showing veins of deeper orange pink. Wings rose, with a strong hint of orange, showing veins of orange rose. Very large size, vigorous. It is the largest and best of all this shade." (LM) "...best described as a salmon pink or salmon red. A first class variety, and worthy of its name." (RS) Strongly scented. Named for the great Victorian and Edwardian gardener. (Eckford, 1900)

'MM' (Spencer)
Bronze pink. Slightly scented. (Grayson, 1999)

'Mollie Rilstone' (Spencer)
Gorgeous pink picotee on cream. Standards cream, picoteed in rose, with the edges rippled; slightly darker behind; tending to arch back. Wings as standards but white with a paler edge; cream below. Some slightly paler. Strongly scented. (Tremewan)

'Molly Cuer' (Spencer)
Bright clear sky blue, with long stems. Strongly scented. Named for the former chair of the Worthing Horticultural Society, England. (Tullett, 1999)

'Monarch's Diamond' (Spencer)
Pink picotee on cream. Well scented. (Unwins, 1987)

'Moorland Beauty' (Spencer)
Large-flowered mauve with well-placed flowers. Slightly scented. (Albutt)

'Moorland Mist' (Spencer)
Vigorous, long-stemmed pale lavender. Well scented. (Albutt)

'Morning Rose' (Spencer)
Very pale pink. Strongly scented. (Kershaw)

'Morven' (Spencer)
Prolific bright cerise. Well scented.

'Mrs Bernard Jones' (Spencer) ♔ 1994
A classic variety, and still superb. Standards well waved, sugar pink, noticeably rayed and white at

'Mrs Bernard Jones'

the edges; paler on the reverse. Wings coloured as the standards, well waved in rolls, paler on the underside. Whole flower pales with age. Large and striking. Well scented. Named for the wife of the great sweet pea breeder. (Unwins, 1981)

'Mrs C. Kay' (Spencer)
Lavender. Once the most popular in its colour and very widely grown. Strongly scented.

'Mrs Collier' (Grandiflora)
A very elegant and dainty, slightly creamy white. Buds yellow. Standards rounded, slightly creamy white, very noticeably creased, some upright but some angled forward; reverse darker, almost primrose. Wings neatly angled down around keel, slightly rolled forward at the sides. Keel cream. Superficially very similar to *Lathyrus latifolius* 'Albus'. Good in heat. "So many are anxious to get a yellow Sweet Pea that anything approaching this colour has all sorts of names." (RS) "Primrose self." (LM) Originally shown as 'Dora Cowper', Sydenham maintains it should be known by that name. Strongly scented. (Dobbie, 1906)

'Mrs Joan Ward' (Spencer)
Clear salmon pink. Strongly scented. (Fred Ward)

'Mrs June Grayson' (Spencer)
Cerise. Well scented. (Grayson, 1997)

'Mrs R. Bolton' (Spencer)
A deep almond pink with large, perfectly formed flowers. An old favourite. (Bolton)

'Mrs Walter Wright' (Grandiflora)
Pretty two-tone purple bicolour. Standards peaked, top edges rolled forward, bases flared back; vivid purple, paler at the lobes, bluish in the centre; reverse duskier. Wings overlapped over the keel, angled down, similar to standards but more blue; paler and bluer below. "It has a fine bold flower, with large hooded standard and well-formed wings; generally three flowers on a stem. The colour is rather difficult to describe; some call it a mauve, but I think it is best described as a rosy-mauve or rosy purple... undoubtedly one of the best and largest of this shade of colour in the old type." (RS) (Eckford, 1902) There was also a 'Mrs Walter Wright Spencer', "a very good waved form of 'Mrs Walter Wright', but unfortunately it is not fixed at present". (RS) And a 'Walter P. Wright'.

'Mumsie' (Spencer)
Vigorous crimson. Slightly scented. (Eagle)

'Myrtle Mann' (Spencer)
Vigorous orange red with pink highlights on stout stems. Strongly scented. (King)

'Nacre' (Spencer)
Cream, flushed with pink. Well scented. (Grayson, 1997)

'Nancy Chisholm' (Spencer)
Rose pink on a white ground. Well scented.

'Nancy Colledge' (Spencer)
Prolific rose with scarlet haze. Opens rather rounded, then slightly ruffled; some flowers duplex. Standards scarlet rose, white at the base, slightly ruffled. Wings more scarlet than rose, paler below, more ruffled. Seven or eight flowers per stem. Strongly scented. (Colledge, 1980)

'Nanette Newman' (Spencer)
Pale carmine pink.

'Nelly Viner' (Spencer)
A very slightly waved uniform pale rose pink. Strongly scented. (Page 10.)

New Century Series (Intermediate)
Spencer-style flowers on plants without tendrils about 1.2m/4ft high. The series comprises nine varieties: 'Aquarius' (lavender), 'Aries' (pink), 'Capricorn' (crimson), 'Gemini' (Appleblossom pink), 'Libra' (pale rose), 'Pisces' (white, flushed pink), 'Sagittarius' (orange), 'Scorpio' (blue), 'Virgo' (white, sometimes with a hint of pink). 'Virgo' is the first Intermediate to receive not only an AGM 1999, but also an AM for Exhibition. (Kings)

'Nimbus' (Spencer)
Captivating inky striped flowers. Standards upright, but with the top rolled back; greyish-white with a bold streak of inky blue-black up the centre; reverse radiating colour, dense in the centre and with black wire. Wings with a dense, deepest purple-black streak over the keel, then an even radiation of colour, with reduced speckling just inside the edge, then purple-black wire. Lasts very well in water. Late, with smaller flowers than 'Tom'. (Unwins, 1996)

'Noel Edmonds' (Spencer)
Rich orange pink. Named for the TV personality.

'Noel Sutton' (Spencer) ♔ 1994
An old favourite and still one of the best blues. Rich colour, vigorous, but tends to be damaged by rain. Well scented. (Suttons)

'Nora Holman' (Spencer)
Exquisite soft rose. Standards upright, pale rose to more or less ivory at the base and edge; slightly ruffled, slightly cream at the edge on reverse. Wings have good form, slightly ruffled, colour as standards, often held up to reveal underside whose colour is the same as the top. Very large early flowers, even on a bush, but not early. Superb for exhibition. Well scented. (Tremewan)

'Norman Wisdom' (Spencer)
Large-flowered white. Buds primrose cream opening to rather pinched standards, broadly waved, pure white with a cream edge and a cream dusting on the reverse. Wings pure white, broadly waved, some cream. (Unwins, 2002)

'North Shore' (Spencer)
Navy blue standard with pale violet wings. Prolific and striking. Strongly scented. (Hammett)

'Oban Bay' (Spencer) ♔ 1997
A lovely well-scented silvery blue. Standards waved, white quickly darkening to silvery blue; wings waved, turned down, colour as standards. Best in cooler areas. Strongly scented. (Chisholm)

'Oklahoma' (Spencer) ♔ 2000
Very dramatic, large-flowered scarlet flake. Buds yellow flushed with red. Standards not waved, or just slightly, and swept back with age. Wings have edges rolled under. Standards and wings densely streaked in deep scarlet, not quite crimson, front and back. Gives a very rich impression. (Unwins, 2002)

'North Shore'

'OLA' (Spencer)
Rosy lavender with long, stout stems. Strongly scented.

'Old English Bouquet Mix' (Spencer)
Long- and stout-stemmed mix of pinks and salmons through to darker lavender shades. Well scented.

'Old Fashioned Flake Mixed' (Grandiflora)
Mixture of old flake types. Strongly scented.

'Old Fashioned Holiday Mixed' (Grandiflora)
Grandifloras in a red, white and blue blend. Strongly scented.

'Old Fashioned Mixed' (Grandiflora)
Mixture of Grandiflora and earlier varieties. Strongly scented.

'Old Spice' (Grandiflora)
Mixture of Grandiflora, and older, varieties. Good in areas with hot summer. Strongly scented. Also known as 'Old Spice Antiques'.

'Old Times' (Spencer)
Cream, soft blue tint. Strongly scented. (Unwins, 1976)

'Oliver Cromwell' (Spencer)
Large-flowered maroon. A brighter, less intense colour than others in this group, but prolific and long-stemmed. (Unwins, 2000)

'Orange Dragon' (Spencer)
Brilliant orange, but appreciates a little shade. Slightly scented.

'Orange Flake' (Spencer)
Reddish-orange streaks on a pink-white background.

'Orange Surprise'
Large, brilliant orange-red with cerise tones. (Kings)

'Oregon Sunset' (Spencer)
Large, long-stemmed flowers in blend of soft pink, cream and orange.

'Original' (Species)
Dr Keith Hammett's 1970s introduction of *L. odoratus* from the wild in Sicily. Short and bushy. Strongly scented.

'Our Harry' (Spencer)
Vibrant blue mauve. Standards strongly reflexed, gently waved, dense lavender blue and paler at the edges. Wings slightly darker, slightly waved, strongly folded down around the white keel which is tinted purple. Slightly scented.

'Our Jenny' (Spencer)
Bright mid-blue.

'Our Joyce' (Spencer)
Sparkling orange rose. Standards a very uniform pale, slightly orange rose, beautifully even on the front and silvered at the top on the reverse; pinched and waved. Wings pale, slightly orange rose, paler towards lip and noticeably paler below. Short, but sun-proof. Strongly scented. (Unwins, 1984)

'Original', the true wild Lathyrus odoratus from Sicily.

'Ouse Valley' (Spencer)
Lavender. Strongly scented.

'Oxford Blue' (Spencer)
Large-flowered rich blue with lavender and occasional reddish tints. Standards well-ruffled, strong lavender blue, delicately veined darker, slightly darker at the centre and lobes; tends to be unbalanced in its waviness; reverse slightly darker. Wings very slightly darker, sometimes a more electric shade, well ruffled though tending to roll under at the edges; reverse same. Long, stout stems. Well scented. (Unwins, 2001)

'Pageantry' (Spencer)
Large-flowered reddish-purple. Slightly scented.

'Painted Lady' (Original)
"...pink standard and white wings; rarely has more than one or two flowers on a stem; a variety of the past." (RS) Modern stocks are usually "improvements" with three or four flowers per stem. Strongly scented. (1731) (Page 6.)

'Pall Mall' (Spencer)
Rich mauve.

'Pamela' (Spencer)
Long-stemmed pale lavender. Strongly scented. (Walker)

'Panache' (Spencer)
Lavender mauve with long stems. Slightly scented.

'Patio' (Dwarf) ♛ 1996
Mixture of dwarf sweet peas reaching 30–38cm/12–15in in height, with stems carrying three or four slightly rippled flowers in shades of red, blue, pink with the addition of some scarlet and white. Well scented. (Pan American)

'Pat Mitchell' (Spencer)
Bright rose pink, with a faint orange overlay, and five or six well-waved flowers per stem. Slightly scented. (Unwins, 1982)

'Patricia Ann'

'Patricia Ann' (Spencer)
Flowers attractively veined with deeper shadings. Named after Patricia Ann Bradbrook, from Adelaide, who won a competition to name a sweet pea.

'Patricia Anne' (Spencer) ♛ 1999
Large-flowered pale lavender. Standards reflexed, waved, white but heavily flushed with lavender though remaining white at the centre. Wings spreading, waved, coloured as standards. Strong scent. (Sutton)

'Peach Sundae' (Spencer)
Red and pink shades. Well scented.

'Peacock' (Spencer)
Standards nicely waved, open silvery white almost flaked in lilac, cream at the edge with a darker reverse; later, bright rosy purple, white at the centre, darker and more even behind. Wings open, slightly messy, more ruffled than the standards but the same colour yet paler below. Keel white, wired in purple. Changes noticeably in

A   'Castle of Mey'
B   'Darcey Bussell'
C   'Martha Lane Fox'
D   'Imogen'
E   'Eileen Brinton'
F   'Valentine'
G   'Valerie Harrod'

colour, the impact of the strong colour of the mature flowers is reduced by the intermingling of paler young flowers. (Unwins, 2002)

'Pearl' (Spencer)
Cream, flushed with pale pink. Well scented. (Grayson, 1997) There was also a 'Pearl' (Bolton) which sounds very similar, awarded an AM in 1959. And a much earlier Spencer 'Pearl': "...too near 'Etta Dyke' to warrant another name". (RS) Of 'Etta Dyke': "...the first white-waved variety of the 'Countess Spencer' type... it is astonishing how soon (this) was found in about a dozen other places and claimed by different raisers as one of their own seedlings." (RS)

'Peerless Pink' (Spencer)
Deep rose pink. (Unwins, 1974)

'Percy Thrower' (Spencer)
Large-flowered and vigorous lavender flush on white. Named for the first British TV gardening personality. Strongly scented. (Bolton)

'Perfume Delight' (Grandiflora)
Heat-tolerant mixture of up to 26 unusually strongly scented varieties. Strongly fragrant.

'Philip Miller' (Modern Grandiflora)
Cerise flecked with deep blue. (Grayson, 1996)

'Phoebe' (Spencer) 🏆 1997
Endearingly variable flake in cerise, red and orange. Standards waved, ivory white at the base, otherwise strongly streaked in cerise, red or orange. Wings turned down, waved, colour as standards. Slightly variable in colour. Slightly scented. (Bolton)

'Pink and White Ripple' (Modern Grandiflora)
Stripe featuring carmine pink markings on a white background. Well scented. (Thompson & Morgan, 2002)

'Pink Bouquet' (Spencer)
Frilly and fragrant warm pink. Standards strong

rose pink, fading paler at lower lobes; gently waved. Wings gently waved, nicely peaked, also fading towards the edges. Strongly scented. (Unwins, 1986)

'Pink Expression' (Spencer)
Large-flowered sugar pink on a white ground. Standards strongly ruffled, white with a hint of cream at the base; veining in sugar pink, even and dense but white ground always shows through; reverse similar. Wings the same only a slightly richer colour; paler below and well ruffled. Some duplex flowers. The tip of the white keel tends to peep through. One of the later pinks. Strongly scented. (Unwins, 1990)

'Pink Flake' (Spencer)
Bright rose pink flake.

'Pink Leamington' (Spencer)
Salmon pink with a cream centre.

'Pink Perfume' (Dwarf)
Ruffled, shell pink flowers. Prolific. Strongly scented.

'Pink Persuasion' (Spencer)
Pink, with a white centre. (2001)

'Pink Reflections' (Spencer)
Mixture of selected varieties from pastel pink to deep rose, both selfs and bicolours. Strongly scented. (Hammett, 2002)

Pinocchio Series (Dwarf)
A recent introduction in the Cupid style. The colours available are: Cherry, Salmon Rose, Purple, Violet and Purple, Red and White, Maroon and White, Carmine and White. (Beane)

'Pip Tremewan' (Spencer)
Bright mauve on long, strong stems. Slightly scented. (Tremewan)

'Pluto' (Spencer)
Deepest navy blue. Well scented.

'Pois de Senteur Sauvage'
See *Lathyrus odoratus* (page 97).

'Potted Fragrance' (Dwarf)
Australian mix of dwarf scented types.

'Powdered Lady'
See 'Painted Lady'.

'Pre-Spencer Grandiflora Mix' (Grandiflora)
Mixture of Grandiflora varieties. Strongly scented.

'Pretty Polly' (Spencer)
Salmon pink with hints of soft orange. Vigorous and sun-proof. (Bolton)

'Prima Donna' (Grandiflora)
Cool pink classic old-fashioned Grandiflora. Standards with sides rolled well forward and held well forward over the wings, pale rose, and increasingly white towards the base; reverse darker, white at the tip. Wings very pale, white with a haze of rose, paler below, strongly rolled round the white keel. Three flowers per stem. "A pale soft pink self; standard hoods a little; usually has three, sometimes four, flowers on a good long stem;... I consider it one of the best of the old type of this colour" (RS) (Eckford, 1896)

'Prince Edward of York' (Grandiflora)
"Bold rosy salmon, some say salmon carmine standard, with rosy wings; a charming combination of colour, usually three, sometimes four, flowers on a stem. Some growers say it loses colour when cut, but this is obviated by adding a little sulphate of iron to the water." (RS) (Eckford, 1897)

'Prince of Orange' (Grandiflora)
"May be described as an orange and rose bicolour, but unfortunately scalds and was not properly fixed in 1910. I see the raiser admits this in her list, but when she states that Holmes's 'Thomas Stevenson' is identical, I think she makes an ungenerous and unwarranted statement, as when I saw 'Thomas Stevenson' it was perfectly true and infinitely superior." (RS) (Hemus, 1910) There was also a 'Prince of Orange' Spencer. (Unwins, 1928)

'Princess Elizabeth' (Spencer)
Salmon pink on a rich cream ground.

'Princess Juliana' (Spencer)
Standards pale rose, very small, creamy at the base; gently and evenly waved, darker on front than on reverse. Wings same as standards, very neatly waved at best, sometimes slightly messy. Slightly scented. (Brewer) There was also an earlier Spencer 'Princess Juliana': "Too near 'Clara Curtis' to warrant another name." (RS) Of 'Clara Curtis': "The first and the best of the waved primrose Spencer type; generally three, or often four, flowers on a stem... it has endless synonyms." (RS)

'Princess of Wales' (Grandiflora)
Very pretty, large-flowered lavender and white. Standards upright but rolled forward at the top of each side and with the base flared back; white,

'Princess Juliana'

'Queen Alexandra'

hazed in mauve; reverse darker and picoteed, picotee visible following the rolling forward. Wings
broad, angled down, rolled inwards, white hazed
with lavender; reverse peachy lavender white. "A
fine bold flower of the old type, with a dull bluish
stripe on a dull white ground; somewhat similar to
'Senator', but more blue in the stripes or markings,
and hoods rather more in the standard. Usually three
flowers on long stems." (RS) (Eckford, 1888)

'Pulsar' (Spencer)
Very pretty pale lavender stripe. Creamy yellow buds
with mauve base. White ground, speckled rich purple though the overall effect is paler. Standards well
waved, wings hardly reflexed under; wire on wings
and back of standards. Strongly scented. Also
known as 'Lilac Ripple'. (Unwins, 1997)

'Purple Flake' (Spencer)
Violet streaks on an off-white background.

'Purple Prince' (Grandiflora)
"Dark marone standard, with dull purple wings; flow-

ers small, of no particular merit." (RS) (Eckford) There
was also 'Purple Prince Spencer'. (Burpee, 1909)

'Purple Velvet' (Spencer)
Rich purple. (Unwins, 1948)

'Queen Alexandra' (Grandiflora)
Very dramatic and vivid. Standards flat, not rounded but noticeably flat-topped, peaked, vivid
carmine-vermilion with a deeper flash in the throat;
reverse more orange. Wings deep carmine rose,
angled over the keel and slightly folded at the front.
"A bright crimson scarlet self... Generally three
flowers on a stem... One of the most popular varieties." (RS) Relatively unbranched so excellent in
shrubs. Sometimes listed as 'Queen Alexander'. Well
scented. (Eckford, 1906)

'Queen Mother' (Spencer)
Unusual freckled white. Buds cream. Standards
crimped and waved, upright, white, streaked
and freckled in salmon orange. Wings slightly
paler than standards, white at the edges; same
below. Keel cream. Some duplex flowers. Relatively
short. Strongly scented. (Unwins, 1991)

'Queen of Hearts' (Spencer)
Prolific and early cerise stripe. Large and evenly
waved flowers. Buds creamy yellow flushed with
dark pink. Standards white, with pale cerise hazing
and wire on the back of the standards, slightly less
dark hazing on the back of the wings; strong
wiring. Effect softer than 'Comet' and with larger
flowers. (Tulett)

'Queen of the Isles' (Grandiflora)
"A very peculiar variety; it has a bright red stripe on
a white ground standard, as in 'America', but the
wings have a clear magenta stripe, a peculiar
colouring seen in no other variety, but as a flower is
of no special merit." (RS) (Eckford, 1885)

'Queen of the Night' (Grandiflora)
Blend of dark shades including navy blue, mauve-
blue, bicolour maroon and lilac, dark crimson and
salmon-pink.

'Quito' (Original)
Maroon standard and mauve wings. Found in the same garden in Peru as 'Matucana', where it was probably introduced by the Spanish, perhaps in the 1920s. Similar to the wild species, 'Matucana', and 'Original'. Strongly scented.

'Rare Melody' (Spencer)
See 'Melody'.

'Raspberry Ice' (Modern Grandiflora)
Bright, but not quite raspberry, red. Standards open pale vermilion then to bright vermilion, ruffled and rippled; some lean forward, some nicely upright. Wings coloured as standard, point varies from a neat V to a ripple. Overall effect bright, but rather muddled. Strongly scented.

'Red Ace' (Spencer)
Large-flowered scarlet, with well-placed flowers. Well scented.

'Red Arrow' (Spencer)
Old favourite in orange scarlet. Standards slightly ruffled, more or less uniform orange scarlet, though paler at the edge; reverse more uniform in colour. Wings

A   'Aquarius'
B   'Queen of Hearts'
C   'Comet'
D   'Queen of Hearts'
E   'Pulsar'

folded well down, same colour as standards, white at the base. Weathers badly, but generally sun-proof. Hardly scented. (Unwins, 1983)

'Red Ensign' (Spencer)
Vivid red, flowers rather small and only slightly waved. Slightly scented. (B. R. Jones)

'Red Ripple' (Spencer)
Dramatic red-striped variety. Standards slightly ruffled, the edges tending to roll back; white, with a faint streaking of purple showing through from behind, and a patch of deep cerise purple at the base in the centre; almost no wire. Wings held down around the keel and rolled under, pale watery cerise with a purple band along the edges over the keel, then a dense radiating pattern of streaking fading into an almost-white zone then a pale wire edge; reverse white with colour showing through from behind. Slightly variable, some rather pale, noticeably more red. Very similar to 'Kyle the Clown', but slightly less rich.

'Regal Reflections' (Spencer)
Two-tone lavender. Well scented. Named in celebration of Her Majesty Queen Elizabeth, The Queen Mother's 100th birthday. Strongly scented. (2001)

'Remembrance' (Spencer)
Deep maroon scarlet. Standards open cerise maroon, darker at the edges, then develop to chocolate purple; slightly ruffled. Wings open as standards, with pale tips, then change to chocolate purple, more scarlet below. Keel mauve. Whole flower slightly ruffled.

'Renaissance' (Spencer)
Dramatic bicolour, deep rose pink standards and palest pink wings. Short. One of the earliest of Keith Hammett's bicolours, awarded an AM in 1977. Well scented. (Hammett)

'Restormel' (Spencer)
Standards broadly waved, very uniform colour, excellent shape, pale orange red with a scarlet picotee; shimmering well on the reverse. Wings broadly waved, with uniform dense scarlet veining,

'Romeo'

paler colour showing through; noticeably veined below. A little late flowering and rather weak, especially compared with 'Garden News', but a better exhibition variety. Resistant to bud drop. Well scented. (Tremewan)

'Rhapsody in Blue' (Spencer)
Blend of blue shades, from very deep blue to pale blue, plus white. (Unwins)

'Richard and Judy' (Spencer)
Softly, rather than boldly contrasting, two-tone effect. Standards evenly waved, soft purple, white at the base; darker behind. Wings broad and falling away at the edges; paler than standards, prettily veined, paler at the edges, slightly silvery and pale below. Keel silvery white with purple edges. Named for the husband-and-wife TV presenters. Exceptionally strongly scented.

'Richard Davey' (Spencer)
Cerise. Slightly scented.

'Robert Uvedale' (Spencer)
Large flowers, very bright and bold. Standards deep carmine, shading to white at the edges, well waved or slightly waved, upright. Wings darker, more or less solid carmine below, less dense colour at the base and edges. Very even and elegant wings. Like a slightly paler version of 'Her Majesty'. Named for Dr Robert Uvedale (page 5). Slightly scented.

'Romance' (Spencer)
See 'Love Match'.

'Romeo' (Modern Grandiflora)
Delightful purple picotee. Buds almost primrose but more or less cream, with purple wire. Standards upright, white with a slightly cream haze, narrowly wired in purple and with neat purple whiskers in the throat; slightly less colour on the reverse. Wings folded downward but as standard in colour, more or less pure white below. Cream keel with a purple tip. Exceptionally pretty but rather short; almost like a small Spencer but with a variable scent. Generally strongly scented. (Unwins, 2000)

'Ron Entwistle' (Spencer) 🏆 1999
Prolific scarlet. Standards reflexed, waved, white heavily flushed with scarlet. Wings spreading, waved, same colour as standards. Slight scent. (Entwistle/Grayson)

'Rosalind' (Spencer)
Gently waved rose pink on a cream ground with a cream keel. Prolific, long-stemmed. Well scented. (Unwins, 1992) There was also a 'Rosalind' Grandiflora: "This I look upon as nothing but another name for 'Marjorie Willis' (see 'Florence') and flowers of that type." (RS) Also two 'Rosalind' Intermediates from King and Burpee.

'Rosanna Alice' (Spencer)
Purple stripe, darker than 'Pulsar'. Well scented. (Unwins, 1995)

'Rosemary Padley' (Spencer)
Deep satiny red with a touch of cherry. Sun-proof and vigorous.

'Rosemary Verey' (Spencer)
Mixture of pink shades with the addition of a rich cream. Named for the influential garden writer. Strongly scented.

'Rosina' (Spencer)
Large-flowered, long-stemmed lavender. Strongly scented. (James)

'Rosy Dawn' (Spencer)
Bright and bold orange-cerise flake. Buds pale cream, hazed in red. Standards hardly waved, cerise radiating on a white ground in a slightly irregular pattern and with a light orange-cerise wire; similar on the back but with no wire. Wings slightly waved, same colours as standards. Overall effect is uniform and striking. Well scented. (Unwins, 1999)

'Rosy Frills' (Spencer)
One of the prettiest of all sweet peas. Buds deep cream, brightly stained in red. Standards white with a sugar pink picotee, hazing to white and richer pink on the reverse; slightly unevenly, but well waved. Wings slightly waved, altogether paler than standards and almost completely white underneath; some duplex. Bright red petioles and red-stained calyx add spark. (Unwins, 1956)

'Royal Baby' (Spencer)
Pretty pale lavender. Buds cream until very soon before flowers open. Standards upright, slightly ruffled, white hazed in lavender with a cream rim, with whiskered white mark at the base; darker on the reverse. Wings as standards, paler below, sides folded down around the keel. Very early but a slightly foggy shade. Strongly scented. (Unwins, 1983)

'Royal Family' (Royal)
Mixture of colours in the Royal Series.

'Royal Flush' (Spencer)
Impressive, very large and well-formed rich cream with a glow of salmon. Well scented. (Bolton)

Royal Series (Royal)
Developed from the Cuthbertsons (page 37), the Royals have stronger stems, larger blooms and more vigorous growth although they flower a little later. Colours are: Blue, Crimson, Lavender, Maroon, Mid Blue, Navy Blue, Rose Pink, Salmon Pink, Scarlet and White. No other varieties with 'Royal' in their name, except 'Royal Family', are connected with this series.

'Royal Velvet' (Spencer)
Blend of rich purple and mauve shades, with some paler tones and white. (Unwins)

'Royal Wedding' (Spencer)
One of the best of all whites. Buds rich creamy yellow. Standards nicely waved, pure white with a hint of cream at the edges and on the reverse and an occasional hint of pink. Wings nicely turned down over the keel, slightly rippled, not

'Royal Family'

rolled under. Very elegant and with long stems, even when grown roughly. Well scented. (Unwins, 1982)

'Roy Castle OBE' (Spencer)
Dramatic strong carmine. Standards open pale cream, deeper at the crease, then open to a more or less uniform shade, strong carmine, very slightly darker at the edge; reverse similar. Wings are the same as standards, paler below. Keel cream, streaked carmine. Bold and pretty, a little late. Named for the singer and cancer campaigner.

'Roy Phillips' (Spencer)
Cerise, flushed with cream.

'Ruby Anniversary' (Spencer)
Large-flowered pale reddish-purple. Standards well-ruffled, cerise purple, reverse paler, more purple at the base. Wings slightly paler, very well ruffled, noticeably paler below. Very striking, and a very uniform colour. Well scented.

'Sally Ann' (Spencer)
Excellent, large-flowered rose on white. Standards nicely ruffled, leaning forward slightly; white at the base, soon a relatively uniform rose though slightly darker at the edge; reverse is the same. Wings same colour, same on reverse, though edges tend to roll under. Well scented. (Brewer)

'Sally Unwin' (Spencer)
Very large, well-shaped flowers; rose pink shading to white at the base. Well scented. (Unwins, 1977)

'Saltwater Taffy Swirls' (Spencer)
Mix of long-stemmed flakes with large ruffled flowers in soft pastel colours, streaked in darker shades. Named for the American seaside confection. Well scented. (2002)

'Sandringham' (Spencer)
Bright scarlet.

'Sara' (Spencer)
Mauve with a silver sheen.

'Sarah Kennedy' (Spencer)
Large flowers, soft rose on white. Standards gently ruffled, especially at the sides, soft rose though darker towards the centre and with a white centre. Wings the same, paler below. Named for the TV presenter. Strongly scented.

'Sea Wolf' (Spencer)
Pale lavender blue flush. Sometimes spelt 'Sea Wolfe'. Strongly scented.

'Selana' (Spencer)
Large-flowered pink picotee.

'Semi-Grandiflora Mixed'
A mixture of varieties whose flowers are between the old Grandifloras and the modern Spencers in size. 'Dragonfly' and 'Kingfisher' are individuals of this type. (Grayson)

'Senator' (Grandiflora)
Pretty two-tone flake. Standards more or less flat,
slightly peaked; white, flaked maroon but slightly purple at the base; reverse much more densely coloured. Wings angled down over keel, white, flaked in purple – a distinct difference in colour between the standards and the wings. Some flowers very densely flaked, between 'Cupani' and 'Senator' in colouring, sometimes with a few 'Cupani' rogues. Two or three flowers per stem. "A striped variety, very much like 'Princess of Wales', but has a chocolate stripe of flake instead of the bluish tinge of 'Princess of Wales', and rather a bolder standard, but where one is grown the other may very well be discarded." (RS) (Eckford, 1891) As is clear, we now grow a slightly different plant. There was also a 'Senator Spencer'. (Morse, 1909

'Sheena' (Spencer)
Two-tone mauve. Hardly scented. (Eagle)

'Sheila Macqueen' (Spencer)
Deep yet bright salmon orange with pink overtones. Vigorous, and sun-proof. Named for the flower arranger and writer. Well scented. (Unwins, 1980)

'Senator'

'Shirley Pink' (Spencer)
Shell pink.

'Sicilian Fuchsia' (Grandiflora)
Pink and cerise bicolour. Strongly scented. Found in Peru and named in honour of Cupani.

'Sicilian Pink' (Grandiflora) 🏆 1995
A delightful darker version of 'Prima Donna'. Standards carmine rose with scarlet flushes, angled forward, paler at the base, peaked, and slightly rolled forward; reverse darker, more carmine, with a white speck at the top as in 'Prima Donna'. Wings pale rose, angled over the keel, paler below. Keel cream. A gorgeous two-tone variety, very pretty. Found in Peru and named in honour of Cupani.

'Silver Jubilee' (Spencer)
Bright orange-cerise on white ground. Well scented.

'Sir Cliff' (Spencer)
Attractive strong mauve. Standards mauve, darkest in the centre, slightly ruffled; reverse the same. Wings slightly darker, paler and slightly silvered below. Keel silvery mauve. Good colour, but not prolific. Named for the singer. Slightly scented. (Unwins, 1999)

'Skylon' (Spencer)
Rose pink, white at the centre.

'Snoopea' (Intermediate)
Spencer-type flowers on Intermediate-sized, tendril-free plants. Wide colour range. Winner of 14 different awards. (King) Superseded by 'Supersnoop'. (Page 89.)

'Snowdonia Park' (Spencer)
White, young flowers flushed with cream. Well scented. (Bailey) There was also a 'Snowdon'. (Unwins, 1937)

'Snow White' (Spencer)
White. Well scented. (Grayson, 1997)

'Solway Fanfare' (Intermediate) 🏆 1996
Widely spaced reddish purple flowers on stout stems; wings and standards both well waved. Slightly scented. (Place)

'Solway Sunset' (Spencer)
Very bright and clean, large-flowered orange-cerise. Buds yellow flushed with red. Standards slightly waved, or flat in the old style, with an occasional rogue in which the sides are slightly rolled; white on front, some red showing through from behind; on the reverse a dense radiation of red (bright, clear and sharp), with a narrow white zone then a neat red line at the edge. Wings strongly rolled under with a rather obvious gap between the two petals over the keel; white, more or less strongly streaked, some very densely, some very dark. Unusually large flowers for a stripe, good colour and long stems. Slightly scented. (Place)

'Sonia' (Spencer)
One of the few marbled types, pale pink with carmine veins.

'Sophie' (Spencer)
Long-stemmed coral pink. Well scented.

'Southampton' (Spencer)
Immaculate, frilly, clear lavender, paling at the edges, on strong stems. Strongly scented. (B. R. Jones)

'South Atlantic' (Spencer)
Hyacinth blue.

'Southbourne' (Spencer) 🏆 1994
Very elegant old favourite in soft rose. Standard upright, ruffled, pinched at the top; opening slightly salmony pink then strong rose pink paling to white at the lobes, hazing to white at the centre; paler on reverse; upright. Wings ruffled, colour as standards sometimes paler below, gently waved. Well scented.

'Souvenir' (Spencer)
Large-flowered deep lavender flushed with rose. (Frances Woodcock)

'Spaceman' (Spencer)
Very pale blue, and without tendrils. Hardly scented. (Grayson, 1997)

A   'W.J. Unwin'
B   'Columbus'   E   'Pink Bouquet'
C   'Daily Mail'   F   'Nora Holman'
D   'Jill Walton'   G   'Royal Wedding'

'Splendour' (Spencer)
Rose pink. There was also a 'Splendour' Grandiflora: "A deep rosy carmine self, with slightly paler wings... Generally three flowers on a stem, but not wanted with the better varieties of recent date." (RS) (Eckford, 1887)

'Starlight' (Spencer)
Fragrant white. Standards waved, white; wings also white but slightly turned down. Strongly scented. (Welch) There is another recent 'Starlight', magenta with a white eye. (Walker)

'Starlight Sonata' (Intermediate) 🏆 2000
Lovely dwarf navy blue stripe. Standards waved, white, densely veined and edged in navy blue; reverse white. Wings waved, white with navy edging and flecks, white with navy wire below. Three to four flowers per stem. Strongly scented. (Place)

'Steve Davis' (Spencer)
Deep cerise with a white keel. Named for the world champion snooker player. Well scented. (Unwins, 1989)

'Streamers'

'Strawberry Ice' (Modern Grandiflora)
Carmine pink. Strongly scented.

'Streamers' (Spencer)
Mixture of flakes. (Hammett, 2002)

'Stripes Mixed' (Spencer)
Scarlet, blue-black, deep crimson, lavender, maroon, rose. A captivating blend, essential. Well scented.

'Stylish' (Spencer)
Mid-blue.

'Subtle Charm' (Spencer)
Large, well-placed pale pink flowers on a white ground. Slightly scented. (Albutt)

'Sunset' (Spencer)
Well-waved, vigorous orange-cerise. Strongly scented. (Harris, 1972)

'Sunset Blend' (Spencer)
Warm pinks, orange and deep reds.

'Sunsilk' (Spencer)
Sun-proof orange pink. (Unwins, 1976)

'Superfine' (Spencer)
Salmon pink on white.

'Supersnoop' (Intermediate)
An improved, earlier 'Snoopea', in eight colours, which is more tolerant of summer heat. (Denholm)

'Superstar' (Spencer)
Deep rose pink, hazing to white at the base. Slightly scented.

'Su Pollard' (Spencer)
Deep rich purple. Named for the comedy actress.

'Swan Lake' (Spencer)
Pure white.

'Sweet Dreams' (Spencer)
Heat-tolerant, bicoloured mixture. Strongly scented.

Sweetie Series (Dwarf)
A series of varieties from Cupid stock specifically selected for use in hanging baskets. The colours are: Carmine, Rose, Cherry, Lavender, Salmon and White. Well scented to hardly scented. (Floranova, 2001)

'Sylvia Moore' (Spencer)
Vigorous rose pink. Well scented. (Albutt)

'Tahiti Sunrise' 🏆 1996
White flowers heavily flushed with red; standards hardly waved, wings well-waved. Strongly scented. (Harrod)

'Tell Tale' (Spencer)
Very pretty lavender rose picotee. Standards open cream, especially on the reverse and broadly picoteed in dark lavender rose, then open white with a hazy picotee which is slightly more extensive on the reverse; tending to fold back strongly and neatly ruffled. Wings also open slightly creamy with a network of dark veins, like butterfly veins, at the edge; then open to pure white with a noticeably less extensive delicate lavender patterning at the edge, or sometimes more extensively; underside paler. Slightly variable, but very pretty.

'Temptation' (Spencer)
Large-flowered and frilly salmon. Good for garden and exhibition. Strongly scented. (1999)

'Teresa Maureen' 🏆 2000
See 'Lavender Bridesmaid' (page 69)

'Terry Wogan' (Spencer)
Prolific warm pink. Buds pale yellowish-green. Standards elegantly and evenly waved, slightly creamy white when first open then strong rose, radiating and filling in from the white centre. Wings more or less evenly and broadly waved, larger creamy white zone than on standards. Rather late. Named for the popular TV and radio presenter. Well scented. (Unwins, 1983)

'The Doctor' (Spencer)
Very pretty well-established old lavender. Standards slightly ruffled. Lavender, darkest in the

'The Doctor'

centre, rolled back at the edges, paler at the sides; cream rim when young; reverse darker. Wings more ruffled, darkly veined on a pale lavender ground; paler and prettily netted below. Vigorous. Strongly scented. (B. R. Jones, 1979)

'The York Pea' (Grandiflora)
Purple-maroon self. (1890)

'Thomas Bradley' (Spencer)
More or less unique rose picotee. Standards ruffled, mainly cream with a dusky dark rose picotee; reverse more strongly veined pink and showing through a little. Wings more ruffled, paler, cream with a gentle rose picotee. Slightly scented. (Unwins, 1995)

'Titan' (Spencer)
Large and frilly pale mauve. Slightly scented.

'Toby Robinson' (Spencer) 🏆 1994
Long-stemmed, well-waved white flowers with pretty purple veining. Strongly scented.

'Tom Cordy' (Spencer)
Soft lilac. Well scented. (Albutt)

A   'Charlie'
B   'Remembrance'
C   'Blaze'
D   'Oxford Blue'
E   'Eclipse'
F   'Ruby Anniversary'
G   'Robert Uvedale'

'Tovah Martin' (Modern Grandiflora)
Mauve and lavender bicolour. Named for the American garden writer. (Grayson, 1997)

'Twilight' (Spencer)
Soft blend of lavender-tinted white, mauve and lavender shades and dusty dark pink.

'Two Tone Mix' (Spencer)
Blend of bold bicolours. Well scented. There was also a well-scented, short 'Two Tone' single colour in reddish-purple and purple. (Hammett)

'Unique' (Spencer)
Lilac pink. (Unwins, 1978) There was also a 'Unique' Grandiflora: "A pale lavender blue stripe on an ivory-white ground. It gives a good medium flower, quite distinct and novel in its markings. Usually two, sometimes three, flowers on a stem." (RS) (Stark)

'Unwins Mixed Stripes' (Spencer)
Superb mixture of striped varieties, including named forms, in scarlet, blue, salmon-rose, lilac, purple and chocolate on cream or white, with varying degrees of waviness. This mixture has been upgraded as breeding has produced better varieties and is substantially different from that sold under this name in the 1980s and before. Strongly scented.

Unwins Striped 'Butterfly' Mix
See 'Unwins Mixed Stripes'.

'Valentine' (Modern Grandiflora)
Delightful and very pretty prolific white. Buds pale greeny cream. Standards folded back on first opening then held relatively flat and very slightly waved, upright, pure white with a slight hint of cream on the reverse; small neat point at the top. Wings gently waved, pure white, folded down over keel. Keel pure white. (Unwins, 2001)

'Valerie Harrod' (Spencer)
Very large but elegant flowers in soft, slightly coral pink. Standards upright, neatly rippled to broadly waved, opening pale rose, more pearly on the back, then becoming stronger rose with a hint of salmon shading to cream at the base and richer at the edge. Wings noticeably darker, increasingly folded over the keel with age, paler below with a large cream zone. Keel cream, tinted pink at the edges. Very neat and striking flower without the blowsinesss of many pinks. Well scented. (Harrod, 2001)

'Vanilla Ice' (Modern Grandiflora)
White. Strongly scented.

'Velvet Night' (Spencer)
Deep blue.

'Vera' (Dwarf/Intermediate) ♛ 2000
A taller and bushier 'Pink Cupid'. Flat, or slightly hooded, pink standards with white wings slightly flushed with pink. Strongly scented. (Levko)

'Vera Lynn' (Spencer)
Standards upright, slightly waved, scarlet rose, shading to silvery white at the base, pale scarlet at the edges with a narrow white rim; paling with age. Wings same as standards but paler beneath, broadly waved, some with a peaked centre, some more rolling. Intended for exhibition. Named for the popular singer. Well scented. (Colledge)

'Violet Queen' (Grandiflora)
"Standard light magenta. Wings lilac. Small size, open form. Standard burns badly with the sun. The wings frequently turn a bright blue when the flower is quite old." (LM) (Carters, 1877)

'Virgo' (Intermediate) ♛ 1999
Award-winning white in New Century Constellation Series (page 75).

'Wedding Day' (Spencer)
Very pretty ruffled white. Opens white with a neat green rim to the standards, then standards well ruffled and tending to fold back; pure white; reverse also white. Wings white top and bottom, tending to fold around the keel. Keel white. Pretty pure white but with a tendency to poor placement of the petals when grown naturally. (Hunt, 2001)

New Sweet Pea "W. J. Unwin"
Raised and introduced by W.J.Unwin, Histon, Cambs 1924.

Above: **The original 'W.J. Unwin' from 1924.**
Below: **'Suttons Avalanche' showing a tendency to**
duplex flowers. Introduced in 1929.

NEW WHITE SWEET PEA.
SUTTON'S AVALANCHE
This wonderful novelty is
described on page 81.
Per packet (30 seeds) · 2s. 6d.
„ (15 seeds) · 1s. 6d.

'Welcome' (Spencer)
Prolific deep red. Well scented. (Unwins, 1932)

'White Ensign' (Spencer)
Pure white.

'White Leamington' (Spencer)
Large, well-frilled, pure white flowers on long stems.
Vigorous. Well scented. (Colledge, 1972)

'White Supreme' (Spencer) 🏆 1994
Very vigorous and long-stemmed, large-flowered
pure white. Excellent for garden, cutting and exhibition. Well scented. (B. R. Jones)

'Willie's Red' (Spencer)
Rich scarlet.

'Wiltshire Ripple' (Spencer)
Rich, dense chocolate-claret stripe on a white back-
ground. Well waved, standards and wings hooded.
Strongly scented. (Wiltshire)

'Windsor' (Spencer)
Chocolate maroon, unusually good in bad weather.
Well scented.

'Wings' (Spencer)
Mauve, good on walls. Excellent garden variety.
Strongly scented.

'Winner' (Spencer)
Scarlet. Hardly scented.

'Winston Churchill' (Spencer)
Well-ruffled bright crimson. Slightly scented. (Cullen)

Winter Elegance Series
Flowering in a day length of just ten hours, so ideal
for climates where the summer sun is too fierce as
they flower in spring. These separate colours are
available: Pink Diana – soft pink with a white base;
Deep Rose – bright pink, almost red; Lavender – soft
lavender; Rose – bright pink; Salmon Cream Pink –
salmon pink with a cream base; Scarlet – bright red;
White – pure white.

Winter-Flowering Series

Four or five scented flowers per stem, flowering from December until weather becomes too warm from August to October sowings. Colours: Crimson, Deep Blue, Lavender, Pink, Rose Crimson, Rose Pink, Salmon Pink, Scarlet and White. For mild winters. Well scented.

'W.J. Unwin' (Spencer)

Bright scarlet rose, lighter than 'Brian Clough'. Standards soft scarlet rose, more refined than 'Nancy Colledge', paler at base and lobes and on reverse. Wings strongly turned down at the sides, otherwise almost flat; same soft scarlet rose and white at the base, paler and rosier below. Pale and hardly ruffled. (Brewer)

'Xenia Field' (Spencer)

Pale blush pink on a cream ground. Well scented. Named for the former gardening columnist of the *Daily Mirror*. (Bolton)

'Yardley' (Spencer)

Soft lavender.

'Yasmin Khan' (Spencer)

Long stems carry large flowers in bright glowing orange-cerise. (Bolton)

'Your Highness'

Strongly scented. (Hammett, 2000)

'Zorija Rose' (Modern Grandiflora)

Very prolific magenta rose. Standards unruffled, sides folded forward; opening pale magenta rose, slightly scarlet in the centre, then becoming powerful bright magenta rose, veined slightly darker, and the same on the reverse. Wings the same, held down over the keel and rolled inwards; same below. The whole flower becomes darker and slightly scarlet with age. Small flowers but prolific and dramatic. Slightly scented. (2001)

'Windsor'

Chapter Eight
Wild annual *Lathyrus*

The genus *Lathyrus* is a member of the pea family, Leguminosae. It contains both annuals and perennials, climbing and bushy; the perennials have sometimes been classified under a separate genus, *Orobus*, but this has not been generally accepted. Most closely related to the vetches, *Vicia*, with which hybrids have occasionally been attempted without success, it has proved impossible to settle on clear-cut differentiating characteristics between the two genera.

There are 164 species of *Lathyrus* spread around the Northern Hemisphere, with a few in South America; the annuals discussed here are predominantly European with a centre of concentration around the Mediterranean. None of the annual *Lathyrus* grown in gardens are native to Britain or North America and many are insufficiently colourful to be of value in gardens. These 11 are worth growing and also available from seed companies, though the more unusual species may take some hunting out.

Lathyrus annuus *L. annuus* L.

Grows in southern Europe, including the Mediterranean countries, eastwards through the Caucasus as far as Iraq and Iran. Generally found in scrub, hedges and stony areas adjacent to cultivated ground. Sometimes grown as a fodder crop.

Growing from 30–150cm/12–60in, the flowers are carried one to three per stem, are about 12–18mm/$\frac{1}{2}$–$\frac{3}{4}$in across, yellow or orange-yellow in colour, or with the standards orange and the wings yellow, often with darker veins. A dainty, pretty, but undramatic species.

'Hotham Red' A red-flowered variant found at the National Collection of *Lathyrus* at Hotham in Sussex. Also known simply as "Red".

'Mrs Rosamund Penney' Orange flowers, often four to a stem.

Lathyrus articulatus *L. articulatus* L.

Grows in the Mediterranean region, plus Portugal. Its habitat is hedges, marginal ground and as a weed of crops.

Growing from 30–100cm/12–40in but taller in gardens, the flowers are carried one to five per stem and are 18mm/$\frac{3}{4}$in across; the standard is deep red, with white or pale pink wings.

Very similar to *L. clymenum*, some authorities consider it insufficiently distinct to be classified separately.

Lathyrus belinensis *L. belinensis* Maxted & Gloyder

Recently discovered in Belen, sometimes spelt Belin, in the extreme south of Turkey near Kumluca in May 1987. This striking new species was found at 560m/1,820ft growing on a rocky limestone hillside and in the margins of cultivated land over one site of about 0.5 sq km (0.193 sq miles). It has now also been found in other sites around Antalya.

Closely related to *L. odoratus*, and almost identical until the flowers open, this new species reaches up to 2m/6ft in the wild. The flowers are similar to those of *L. annuus* but larger and brighter: usually with three to five flowers per stem, the standards 20–26mm/$\frac{3}{4}$–1in, orange-yellow with striking red veining, the yellow falls are about two-thirds of the size.

A pretty and colourful container climber and also being used to develop yellow and, unexpectedly, brilliant blue sweet peas.

Lathyrus chloranthus *L. chloranthus* Boiss.

Grows in India, central Asia, Iraq and Turkey, in scrub, at the edges of woods, and in and around rough fields.

Reaching 70cm/28in in height in the wild, and twice that in gardens, the flowers are carried two or

Above: One of the descendants of L. belinensis, a sparkling red and white bicolour.
Below: Lathyrus sativus.

three per stem, are up to 25mm/1in across, and are an attractive greenish-yellow, sometimes with a small red mark on the standard.

This is a vigorous, bushy and well-branched species with an unusually long flowering period. Good in large containers, it is perhaps best in a Mediterranean garden where it can scramble up the surrounding fence or into stout and well-established shrubs. I have also grown it tumbling down from a sunny, stone-fronted raised bed where it made a mass of long flowering stems. One of the best of these species.

'Lemonade' Generally thought to be nothing more than a selling name for the species, I have not seen it showing the red mark mentioned above, so the name could be valid for unmarked forms.

Lathyrus clymenum *L. clymenum* L.

Growing wild in the Mediterranean region of Europe and North Africa, *L. clymenum* is found as a weed of undeveloped agriculture, in hedges and sometimes near water.

In the wild it grows to about 1m/39in in height, but can be as tall as 1.5m/5ft in gardens, with up to five flowers per stem, each 18mm/³⁄₄in across and crimson in colour, with violet or lilac wings; pale yellow flowers have very occasionally been reported.

This is a delightful and very pretty, though small-flowered, species and another best in the wild of a Mediterranean-style garden than grown more formally on tripods or in annual borders.

'Articulatus' Maroon and white bicolour. (And see L. articulatus, page 94.)

'Chelsea' Lavender-mauve.

L. gorgoni *L. gorgoni* Parl.

Growing wild over a wide area from Sardinia, Sicily and Cyprus in the east, through the eastern Mediterranean to Turkey, Palestine, Iraq and Iran.

Usually found in more moist habitats than most species, including ditches, water meadows and damp fields.

A low scrambler to about 60cm/24in with a single, relatively large, rusty yellow flower, 18–25mm/³⁄₄–1in, on each stem.

A pretty, relatively short, species.

Lathyrus hirsutus *L. hirsutus* L.
Hairy Vetchling

Grows wild over a wide area of central and southern Europe and east through the Caucasus to Afghanistan; usually found in sparsely grassy places, on the undisturbed edges of cultivated fields and amongst sparse scrub.

Grows to 1.2m/4ft in the wild, a little more in gardens, with up to three small flowers, usually no more than 15mm/⁵⁄₈in in size, in red, with pale blue wings. As the name implies, the whole plant is covered with a sparse down.

Not a showy plant, but nevertheless excellent sprawling through low shrubs.

Lathyrus ochrus *L. ochrus* (L.) DC.

Native to the countries surrounding the Mediterranean, *L. ochrus* grows in uncultivated fields, the edges of scrub and woods, roadsides and the sunny banks of ditches.

Reaching about 1m/39in in height, this sprawling species has usually only a single flower per stem, but this flower is bright pale yellow or sometimes a creamy white. The pods are unusual in featuring two wings.

Interesting rather than flamboyant and a pretty scrambler for the sunny wild garden.

Lathyrus odoratus *L. odoratus* L.
Sweet Pea

The species from which all garden sweet peas have been developed.

Native to Sicily and the southern tip of the Italian mainland, where it grows in scrub and roughly cultivated areas. Also naturalized in other parts of southern Europe, in South America and other areas where garden sweet peas have been cultivated.

Reaching up to about 2m/6ft, though often much less, with up to three powerfully scented 20–35mm/³⁄₄–1¹⁄₂in flowers per stem, the colour is maroon in the standards and mauve in the falls. A yellow-flowered form has been reported from Iraq but this has not been confirmed.

'Original' or 'Cupani Original' is the recently collected wild form.

Lathyrus sativus *L. sativus* L.
Chickling Pea

The native origin of this dainty little pea is unknown but it has long been cultivated as a fodder plant and is now naturalized over much of central, southern and eastern Europe, south west Asia and north Africa.

Reaching about 90cm/3ft, but usually less, the flowers are carried singly and are most commonly a bright sky blue but may also be blue with a pink reverse, white, or white with blue wings and a reddish mark on the standards; there are said to be pure pink and also violet forms.

A very pretty plant developing a tangled bush of slender stems covered with flowers for a long period. Good tumbling over a low wall.

'**Albus**' White flowers.
'**Azureus**' Blue flowers. A useful, though possibly redundant, name.
'**Albo-azureus**' White, flecked with blue.
'**Choice Mixed**' A mixture of all shades.

Lathyrus tingitanus *L. tingitanus* L.
Tangier Pea

Native to Portugal and Spain, the Azores, the Canary Islands, Sardinia, Algeria and Morocco, the Tangier pea grows in forest clearings, along hedges, in scrub and scree, and on the edges of cultivated ground.

Reaching 1.2m/4ft, more in gardens, with striking winged stems, at 20–30mm/³⁄₄–1¹⁄₄in the flowers are the largest of any except *L. odoratus* and are held up to three on a stem. The flowers are bright magenta purple with an upright, flat standard but tend to remain closed until midday.

'**Roseus**' Pale pink flowers with reddish mark in the centre of the standard.
'**Harmony**' Larger pink and white bicoloured flowers.
'**Choice Mixed**' Mixture of all shades.

Chapter Nine
Raising sweet peas from seed

Sweet peas are annuals, raised from seed, and are one of the easiest of all seeds to grow. They are large and easy to handle, and almost every seed you buy will be healthy, viable and ready to spring into growth: given moisture and warmth they germinate readily and grow without too much intricate preparation. So, if the fancy takes you, you can ignore most of what follows and jump straight to the quick guide (page 104).

There are, however, some aspects of seed-raising technique which prompt disagreement or which vary in different climates and in different situations. Should the seed be sown in autumn or spring? Should it be chipped to hasten germination? Is there an advantage in soaking or chitting the seed before sowing? Should it be sown in large pots, in smaller individual pots or in the open ground? What is the best compost?

So although it is true that you can simply poke the seeds into the garden with your finger and they will come up, for the very best results a little more care is required.

Autumn or spring?

The sweet pea is an adaptable plant. In the wild, *Lathyrus odoratus* and other annual species tend to behave as winter annuals. Seed germinates in the autumn, the cool moist winter then encourages slow top growth but during this time the roots develop, reaching down towards the subsoil. Then, as the light intensifies and the temperature rises in spring, top growth accelerates. Root growth also increases and, starting from an established root system, can delve deeper in search of moisture reserves as rainfall decreases to almost nothing and the heat of the sun causes increasing evaporation from the leaves.

In spring the plants flower, then in the dry air of summer the seeds ripen. The pods dry, then split and twist with a snap, flinging out the seeds. The hard seed coat protects the seed from drying out in the heat of the summer and as the autumn rains begin, the seed coat softens and germination begins.

In the garden, sowing in the autumn encourages the same early root development. The result is early flowering, a longer flowering period, longer flower stems, more flowers on a stem and also larger flowers – and the plant is usually altogether healthier and more productive. This all arises from the increased flow of moisture and nutrients from the expansive root system. Most exhibitors of sweet peas rely on this approach while gardeners have tended to leave sowing until spring; this also works well but, where the climate allows, autumn sowing can be enormously beneficial for gardeners, too.

It is usual for autumn sowing to be in pots, the young plants overwintered, and planting to be in

Lathyrus articulatus

spring. Planting time for autumn-sown plants is also sowing time for spring-sown plants so it is clear that the former have a significant head start. Of course, it is also possible to sow outside, in the open ground, in the autumn in mild climates.

Sowing in autumn

Sowing in the autumn, in pots, with the protection of a cold frame, well-ventilated cold greenhouse or a sheltered porch, is ideal in most of Britain. October and November are the usual months for autumn sowing; September is too early. It is also good in zones 7 and 8 in the United States and elsewhere; in zones 9 and 10 protection is unnecessary.

Autumn sowing, in the open ground, is possible in much of Britain and up to zone 8 in the USA. This was usual years ago when seed was cheap and plentiful. In much of California, Florida and other hot-summer states (page 129), and of course the Mediterranean and other areas with a similar climate, autumn sowing is the only sensible course. The summer heat and light intensity are unsuitable for sweet peas but autumn sowing will ensure earlier flowering so they will naturally peak before temperatures become intolerable.

In areas with very cold winters and very hot summers, autumn sowing, in the open ground or in pots, is helpful to ensure that flowering peaks before the heat becomes destructive; and in many areas spring is compressed and the transition from winter to summer is brief. But protection from the ferocity of winter is also essential so it is in these areas that growing sweet peas requires more thoughtful consideration, and protection for pot-grown seedlings is essential; a sun room is often the perfect location.

Sowing in spring

In all of Britain, and in many areas of the United States, spring sowing works perfectly well; it also fits in well with the sowing regime for other annuals. Plants give a delightful display, especially if the site is well prepared, and most gardeners are very pleased with the results. Even if you don't have a cold frame or any other protection, sowing in pots is still better than sowing in the open ground.

In Britain some growers sow in pots in January or February, while others wait until March or April; earlier is better as this allows larger plants to be set out giving them the edge on plants grown from seeds sown in the open ground. Even sowing in pots which are set in a sunny sheltered corner, rather than in the additional protection of a cold frame or cold greenhouse, brings the advantage of good compost and, presumably, regular watering.

In areas of the United States with cold winters and warm summers, growth from a spring sowing, carried out as soon as the snow and frozen soil have thawed, can be very rapid and can give a dazzling display.

Sowing in the open ground in spring, in long rows for cutting, was once the usual method in the days when seed was inexpensive and there were often staff to help with the care and cultivation.

Late spring sowings

It is often forgotten that sowing in late spring in much of Britain can also work well. Seed can be sown in the open ground, although it's often more convenient to sow in pots at a time of year when the borders should be bursting with plants. Sowing in May or early June will bring flowers in late summer and early autumn, when the flowering of earlier plants is over and the plants removed.

This is successful in much of Britain, and in the Pacific Northwest, although less so in areas with short cool summers, and in many other areas where the summers are warm but not hot.

Sowing technique

Most bought seed is grown in a climate and in a way that ensures that the germination potential is very high – 100 per cent is not uncommon – so you might think that all you have to do is fling it out into the garden and up it will jump. But although the seed may be viable, it still needs the right conditions to ensure that it grows.

Choosing seeds Bought seed is always preferable to home-saved seed. This may sound heretical to the enthusiasts for heirlooms for whom saving seed from the garden is seen as an important safeguard.

But when seed develops in the uncertain environment of the home garden, especially in cool damp summers, it may not boast the high viability of seed grown by specialist seed growers. In addition, home gardeners may not notice unwanted variations in colour, vigour or productivity which seed producers remove from among the plants from which they collect seed. If seed is collected from these rogues (or off types) the unwanted characteristics may reappear, more noticeably, in the following year's plants.

So buy seed from sweet pea specialists or from seed companies which include a good range of sweet peas among their more general offering (page 137).

Chipping and sanding Most sweet peas have a hard seed coat to prevent the seed drying out during the hot summer in the areas in which they grow wild. This works to the advantage of wild species in another way. Not all of these hard-coated seeds may soften in the autumn rains so, while many will germinate, others may not – but they will probably germinate after a further soaking in the following year, or the year after. So the whole of any one season's seeds will rarely germinate at the same time. This has obvious advantages in the wild: if bad weather, insect damage or some other natural mishap wipes out all of one season's seedlings, there are still seeds left in the soil to produce a new generation of plants the following year.

But gardeners need all their seeds to germinate at once. To ensure that they all take up water and germinate together, which is especially convenient when sowing in pots, it helps to break through the hard seed coat to ensure that moisture can penetrate. This can be done in a number of ways:

Seeds can be spread on a piece of sandpaper, then a second sheet laid over the top and rubbed over the seeds to wear through the seed coat. I find this tedious and not altogether successful.

Some gardeners use a large nail clipper to make a nick in the seed coat but while some seeds are slightly nobbly and have edges which can conveniently be clipped off, most are much more rounded, making this a more tricky proposition.

My preference is to use a knife or a nail file or a small triangular wood file, although all can be hard on the fingers. Gripping an individual seed between thumb and forefinger of the weaker hand, use a sharp knife (the force required by a blunt knife is more likely to cut you) to make a nick in the seed coat. A new nail file, or wood file, run once or twice across the seed, will also usually make an abrasion sufficient to allow water to penetrate.

Some growers treat every seed in this way before sowing. Others soak the seed first.

Soaking seeds The simple way of doing this is to line a small plastic box (a used margarine tub is ideal) with moist kitchen paper, lay the seeds out on it, replace the lid and stand the box in a warm light place. The paper must be moist but not soggy, the site should be warm (7–18°C/45–65°F) but not hot.

In a matter of hours most, perhaps all, of the seeds will swell, indicating that they have taken up water and the germination process has begun. The size difference is quite clear. At this stage seeds which have not swollen can be removed, nicked with a knife or file and replaced on the damp sheet. These too will then usually swell. The seeds are now ready for sowing. They can be left for a day or two, but the root will soon start to emerge, especially in warm conditions, and the seed should be sown promptly once the root is visible. Taking the process to this stage is called chitting.

A simpler, but riskier, alternative is to fill a cup or saucer with warm water and leave the seed to soak overnight in a warm room. Most will take up water and swell noticeably by morning and can be sown; the remainder can be nicked and put back in the water where they will often swell up quickly. The danger is that if the seeds are left floating in the water for too long, they may start to rot; there is a greater margin for error with seeds lain on damp paper.

Labelling At this stage the seeds should be labelled. It is convenient simply to write a label noting the variety name and the date before you open each packet. By writing neatly it is also possible, over the season, to record on the label the dates of germination, planting out, first flowering and so on, and a reminder to grow the same variety again the following year (or not, as the case may be); the label can then be kept as a record – few of us can boast the discipline to record such information in a book.

'Colin Unwin'

Sowing in protection

There are a number of alternative strategies available in terms of location, pots and composts. The approach depends on the facilities available, personal preference and experience.

Which pots? Traditionally sweet pea seeds were sown either in 12.5cm/5in clay pots or in individual open-bottomed sweet pea pots made of bitumized paper; both are now outdated. The three modern alternatives are large plastic pots, small plastic pots and plastic modules.

For many years I used 12.5cm/5in plastic pots, with six seeds sown in a ring towards the edge. For planting alongside individual canes or along a length of netting the plants were broken from their collective root ball and planted as individuals; alternatively, the whole pot could be planted inside a

vertical wire tube or under a shrub or climber for less-controlled growth.

The advantages of sowing in large pots are the likelihood that such pots are already to hand, and the relative ease with which a large mass of compost can be handled and kept moist. When planted as a whole, root disturbance is minimal although, when planted as individuals and the root ball broken up, some root damage is inevitable – but the effect is so small as to be noticeable only to purists.

Small, 7.5cm/3in or 9cm/3½in pots are also useful; again they are often to hand and can be used for sowing individual seeds, but the restricted depth is not really suitable for plants with such deep-questing roots – the result is often that roots curl around the base of the pots. Such pots are best for Dwarf and Intermediate varieties with their more limited root growth, and three seeds of 'Cupid', 'Pinocchio' or 'Sweetie' are ideal sown in a 9cm/3½in pot.

Plastic modules, in particular Rootrainers, the successor of the old sweet pea pots, are definitely the preferred choice for the serious sweet pea grower. A single seed is sown in each tall, slender, re-usable module, which splits to allow plants to be removed easily for planting and which can then be washed and re-used. Their deeper root run is an advantage, as is the fact that they come as part of a simple system in which the modules are suspended from a plastic frame so the base of the pots is not resting on a tray. The result is what is known as 'air-pruning' – as roots start to emerge from the base of each module, exposure to the air causes growth to cease and the roots to throw out branches higher up in the pot. The resulting well-branched root ball is then poised to develop strongly when planted.

Sowing compost This is another contentious point. Many growers obtain excellent results by using peat-based seed-sowing or multipurpose compost or a peat-free alternative. If using peat-free composts, always run a small trial alongside your usual compost before changing to the new formulation, as peat-free composts behave very differently from peat composts, especially in terms of water and nutrient requirements; they cannot be managed in exactly the same way.

For sowing in the autumn I prefer to add some drainage material such as perlite to counter the possibility of waterlogging, especially if the pots are stood in a sheltered corner outside, exposed to rain and

'Rosemary' (left) and 'Gloria' on the cover of the Unwins Autumn 1934 catalogue.

snow, rather than in the protection of a cold frame or cold greenhouse. Three or four parts of compost by volume well mixed with one part of perlite is about right. Adding drainage material does, however, dilute the nutrients in the compost and, anyway, these nutrients are usually only intended to be sufficient for about six weeks of growth, so supplementary feeding will be necessary. Slow-release granules are one possibility, although the release of nutrients from the granules is controlled by temperature and, in the cool of the autumn and early spring, little may be released. Liquid feeding with a specialist sweet pea food (if still available) or tomato food is usually preferable.

Many growers still use loam-based John Innes compost for sowing. This provides a longer-lasting reservoir of nutrients and many growers believe that

plants grown in John Innes compost settle in more quickly. But be aware that the quality of John Innes composts available in garden centres varies enormously; if you find a brand whose quality is dependably good, use it – otherwise steer clear.

Sowing the seed Ensure that your compost is moist, but not soggy. Fill the pots, whichever type, to the rim, then tap them on the table or bench to settle the compost. Very gentle firming to remove any air pockets is also helpful but forceful use of the fingers should be avoided as overcompacting the compost can dramatically reduce the drainage potential. When using round pots, gentle firming with the base of another pot is usually the simplest method; few gardeners will want to go to the trouble of making a presser, though a circular piece of plywood, cut to the right size and screwed to a short length of dowel, is very useful.

Sweet pea seed is sufficiently large to be handled individually. My approach is to make a hole for each seed using the flat top of a pencil. It is probably unnecessarily fussy, but if you make the hole with the point of a dibber or pencil, the seed may sit suspended over the narrowing base of the hole and not take up moisture readily. (I suspect that this attitude is a side-effect of years of sowing seeds a great deal more demanding than sweet peas, for which conditions must be perfect, and more crucial to my own contentment than the germination of the seeds themselves.)

The depth of the hole is not crucial; the large food reserves in sweet peas ensure that they can cope with deeper sowing than anyone is likely to attempt. There was a time when sowing 10cm/4in deep was recommended: 2.5cm/1in is about right. Drop a seed into each hole, tap the pot on the bench or table again to settle the compost and, if necessary, stir the compost around with the point of a pencil to fill any depressions, then add a little extra if necessary.

Label the pot, add the date of sowing, and water in well with a rose on the watering can. Using soaked or chitted seed followed by a thorough watering will ensure that the germination process continues unchecked.

Place the pots either in a cold greenhouse with

plenty of ventilation, in a cold frame with the lid set ajar, in a cool sun room, or in a sheltered place outside. It is important that the compost does not become too soggy. Autumn-sown seed pots, stood outside on a slab or other hard surface, often become too wet if not raised up to allow water to drain away. A gravel bed can be improvised using a surround of bricks or timber to keep an inch of gravel in place and the pots stood on it; this is the preferred solution for smaller pots. Rootrainers can simply be stood in their frame.

Autumn sowings in greenhouses and frames should be stood on gravel or on a slatted bench and kept well ventilated; they will not be damaged by a light frost but in severe weather ventilators should be closed as protection. Gardeners in very cold areas may need a greenhouse with a heater to keep out the worst of the frost.

Sowing on the windowsill is also an option, especially for dwarf types. In this situation the best approach is probably to use Rootrainers or modules, sets of pots 2in/5cm square connected together to fit neatly into a seed tray for support. The main problem with sowing on a windowsill is that light comes only from one direction. This can be partially remedied by turning the tray every day but tall climbing types are still apt to become too lank and their roots too constricted; the resulting plants will be poor.

Spring sowings, on the other hand, must be kept cool. If raised in a greenhouse alongside half-hardy annuals, which need warm temperatures, growth will be leggy and lank. Maximum ventilation with no additional heat is crucial to ensure the development of a strong root system without encouraging over-vigorous top growth.

Sweet pea seeds and seedlings are favourite food for a number of creatures including slugs (page 121) and especially mice (page 118) which may be the cause of otherwise unexplained germination failure.

After germination
The first sign of germination will be that a slender pointed shoot will emerge. Simplified leaves will then unfurl and side shoots will start to break towards the base. The extent to which side shoots develop varies with the type and the growing conditions. It is customary to pinch out the main shoot to encourage strong side shoots – especially as the main shoot usually weakens and dies as side shoots take over.

Watering The aim from this stage onwards should be to keep the pots consistently moist so there is no check to growth through shortage of water. However, overwatering can result in seeds, or later roots, rotting. Reluctance to overwater, however, should not prevent the pots from receiving a good soak; cautious watering, in which only the top half of the compost in the pot is dampened, will discourage roots from making full use of the depth of the compost.

Feeding Feeding during these early stages is beneficial, especially if the compost used is a standard commercial seed-sowing or multipurpose compost. Use a liquid tomato feed or specialist sweet pea fertilizer, but never overfeed. Autumn-sown plants grow slowly for many months and the aim should not be to force them into untimely vigorous growth but rather to ensure that they never go short of the nutrients they require. The nature of the season and prevailing weather conditions should be your guide: feed only when conditions are naturally likely to encourage plant growth.

Spring-sown plants must be kept growing consistently and so regular feeding, every two weeks, is beneficial. Again, ensure that the compost is thoroughly soaked.

Pinching out and planting
When the seedlings of all but Intermediate and Dwarf types are about 7.5cm/3in high, they should be pinched out to encourage the development of side shoots; these shorter types can be left unpinched.

A simple nip between thumb and forefinger, just above a leaf joint, is sufficient. Two or three side shoots will now surge up from the base and when these are about 7.5–10cm/3–4in high, and still self-supporting, is the time for planting out. Leave it longer and not only will the roots become restricted but the shoots will tend to flop and require support, and continuous strong and sturdy growth will be disrupted.

Sowing outside

While it is undeniable that sowing in pots produces the best plants, it is not actually necessary. Sowing directly into garden soil, in autumn or spring, depending on the climate in your area, can also give impressive results. In general, however, spring sowing is preferable except in areas with mild, equable winters. In heavy clay soils, autumn sowing in the open garden is also likely to be less successful.

Preparation and sowing The soil for sowing should be loose and crumbly, 'friable' being the traditional word. This is achieved by lightly forking over the area, working in some organic matter such as old potting compost, the contents of last season's growing bags, or soil improver from the garden centre. Tread, rake level then rake in some fertilizer.

My approach is to use a dibber and simply make a series of small holes about 25mm/1in deep and drop a seed into each. To be doubly sure of avoiding gaps, sow in two holes side by side at each site; this is also a useful approach when sowing seed of mixtures as it ensures a more complete blend of colours.

The sowing sites should be 15–23cm/6–9in apart along a row of netting, or at the foot of individual canes, depending on the method of support. It is a mistake to sow too closely as, although more plants will result, competition is also increased and, in the end, there will be fewer flowers. Cover the seeds with soil then water in thoroughly with the rose on the watering can. If you have sown chitted seed, add some liquid feed to the water to ensure that plenty of dissolved nutrients are available to the new roots at once. Protect the seeds against mice, slugs and pigeons and ensure that the seeds and new seedlings do not dry out as they become established.

Sweet peas from cuttings

Yes, that's right – cuttings. Decades ago this technique was sometimes used as a way of increasing stock of new varieties or to make more plants when a sowing unexpectedly germinated poorly. Seedlings are pinched out in the normal way, then the resulting young shoots snipped off and rooted when they are about 7.5cm/3in long. They can be treated in much the same way as spring cuttings of perennials, rooted in a 50:50 mix of peat and perlite in a propagator with bottom heat of about 70°F/21°C. They should root in two to three weeks, and can then be moved into pots and grown on before planting out. But remember, always leave at least one shoot on the original seedling so that it can develop. Unfortunately, shoot tips from older plants will not root.

Quick guide to sowing sweet peas

Sweet peas are tough flowers with large, easy-to-handle seeds packed with reserves of food. They can be sown in spring or autumn, inside or out, and it is more difficult to stop them growing than it is to let them flourish.

1. Always buy fresh seed from a sweet pea specialist. Don't save your own seed or use seed from a friend's garden.
2. Sow in autumn or spring in most of Britain (autumn if you need really good plants for arranging or for showing), autumn in areas of the US with mild winters and spring in areas of Britain and the US with cold winters.
3. Sow indoors in early spring in areas of the US with hard winters swiftly followed by hot summers.
4. Soak the seeds on damp kitchen paper overnight to encourage them to take up water quickly.
5. Sow six seeds in a ring towards the edge of a 12.5cm/5in pot of fresh seed compost.
6. Alternatively, sow outside in well-prepared soil where you'd like them to flower but prepare the soil thoroughly and get supports in place first.
7. Label the pot or site with the variety and sowing date.
8. Protect the seeds from slugs, mice, pigeons and waterlogging.
9. Pinch out the tips (or snip them off with the kitchen scissors) when the seedlings are 7.5cm/3in high.
10. Plant when the sideshoots have developed, usually six to eight weeks after a spring sowing.

Chapter Ten
Care and culture of sweet peas

Raising sweet peas is not especially diffi-cult, and once they are planted out they are largely amenable and without unrea-sonable demands. Growing them to exhi-bition standard may require experience, good grow-ing technique and an awareness of their foibles and how to cope with them. But, for the vast majority of gardeners, good garden performance is attainable with attention to a few simple requirements and by considering their needs in the same way as those of other plants in the garden.

Situation

Sweet peas like sunshine. They grow out in the open in the wild and they enjoy a sunny, open position in the garden. There is a caveat to that, though. There is a difference between the overhead shade of tall trees, which is to be avoided, and the shade from the side of a fence or wall, which can be advantageous.

Under trees sweet peas are a disaster: there is just not enough light. Trained on a wall or fence which is open to the skies but upon which the sun rarely shines directly is a good position for garden sweet peas; in fact many scarlet and orange varieties will retain their colour well and all varieties will hold their flowers for longer when grown out of the scorch of the sun.

Soil

Rich, well-drained soil... a nice friable loam... In fact, sweet peas can be grown well in all soils although, in those such as heavy clay and gravel, some improvement through the addition of organic matter will be needed.

In the wild, sweet peas and other *Lathyrus* species tend to fade in late spring and early summer as the temperature and light intensity increases. In the garden we aim to keep them growing right through this period and to do this they need a con-stant water supply and sufficient nutrients to pre-vent them slowing down for as long as possible.

Organic matter is the key to this, and the fact that the roots have the capacity to grow deeply into the soil. Organic matter holds moisture and, in conjunction with organic or inorganic fertilizer, provides nutrients. So the idea is to ensure that there is sufficient organic matter at a depth where the roots can use it, combined with additional watering and feeding when necessary; sweet peas will then provide continuity of colour rather than a single dramatic burst of flowers followed by a sad decline.

So, suppose a row of sweet peas grown on net-ting is planned: first, dig a trench about 30cm/12in across (double that if you need the exercise), so that the line of the netting runs along the middle. The trench should be as deep as your digging spade. Then fork over the bottom of the trench to the depth of your digging fork until the soil is loose and spread a layer of about 7.5cm/3in of organic matter on the top. This can be well-rotted compost or horse manure, composted bark or planting mix from the garden cen-tre – whatever you can lay your hands on as long as it is fine and friable. Fork this into the bottom of the trench thoroughly and tread the soil to remove air pockets. Partially refill the trench with soil, add another 5–7.5cm/2–3in of compost and fork this into the upper layer. Tread this, too, leaving the trench 2.5–5cm/1–2in below the surrounding soil level.

When planting on a circular wigwam of canes the approach should be the same, digging a round hole rather larger than the diameter of your intended wigwam and, again, leaving a depression. If you intend to plant on a narrow vertical cylinder of wire as support, the preparation should be the same but the area scaled to match the site.

This preparation can be done at any conven-ient time in autumn, winter and early spring as long as it is ready in time for spring sowing or planting.

Of course, this is a counsel of perfection... if you wish to avoid forking over the base of your trench, to dig only a narrow trench, or dig no trench at all and simply fork over the area, this will not guarantee disaster: your sweet peas will only be a little less good. If you just want to plant one potful, or only a couple of plants, under a shrub or in front of a hedge, and thorough preparation is impossible owing to the congestion of nearby roots, the competition from these roots makes at least a minimum of preparation even more necessary, so do as much as you can within the constraints of the situation.

Hardiness

Sweet peas and other annual *Lathyrus* species originate in the Mediterranean region where the winters are mild and damp and the summers are hot and dry. They will, however, take light frosts and will tolerate some summer heat if kept moist; they dislike high summer humidity.

In Britain we have the best of all worlds. Young plants will often overwinter outside in the garden in many areas, slugs usually being a greater menace than cold, but the simple precaution of growing them in pots and protecting them in a sheltered corner, in a cold frame or cold greenhouse will ensure they sail through the winter. British summers are rarely so hot that sweet peas are uncomfortable, especially as even if rain is in short supply watering can make up the deficit.

In the United States, things are different (page 129). It is encouraging that sweet pea seedlings will survive if their roots are frozen although prolonged exposure to very cold conditions will kill them. No studies have been done to show exactly what they will tolerate, but in areas colder than USDA zone 8 it would be worth experimenting with overwintering a potful of seedlings or a clump in the garden to discover what they will withstand.

Planting

There is no special mystery to planting sweet pea plants. It helps to rake in some fertilizer – bonemeal at a handful per square yard (60gm/2oz per sq metre/yard) is about right – and water the plants in their pots with a liquid feed the day before planting to encourage them to settle quickly. Then they can be carefully knocked out of their pots. If a whole potful of seedlings is being planted together, dig the hole first – I use what is known as a boy's spade, whose short, narrow blade is ideal for planting, but any trowel or spade will suit. On the assumption that the soil is well prepared, simply plant in the normal way and leave a slight depression afterwards.

If the root ball is to be split and the seedlings planted individually, knock them out of their pot and gently pull the individual plants apart using your fingers. It is inevitable that a few roots will break but the plants will soon recover. Try to keep as much compost on the roots as possible, dig a hole with a trowel, slide in the plant, and firm gently; leave the plant just a little lower in the soil than it was in the compost in its pot.

Water in thoroughly, with some liquid feed in the water, then mulch. Any weed-free organic matter will do – so garden compost is probably unsuitable unless you are a composting wizard and ensure your heap heats up well. Use the contents of old growing bags, carefully broken up, or composted bark or other bagged mulch from the garden centre.

Support

This is sometimes presented as a contentious issue, but really it's not. There are nine basic forms of support: canes in a cordon, canes in a wigwam, netting in a line, netting in a tower, netting on a wall or fence, brushwood, purpose-made supports, other plants – and none at all.

Exhibitors grow their sweet peas as cordons on a row of canes (page 108). Gardeners looking for cut flowers or a dazzling display in the garden more often use canes in a wigwam – six to eight canes, each 2.4m/8ft long, pushed 45cm/18in into the ground in a circle about 90cm/3ft across and their tops pulled together. The tops can be tied with string, or purpose-made plastic disks are available with notches into which canes are locked.

This arrangement provides solid support but has two flaws. The canes themselves rarely provide quite enough early support, and so plastic netting can be wrapped around the outside of the canes, low down, to provide extra support to which tendrils can cling in the first weeks after planting. Another way of providing early support is to set 60cm/2ft lengths of brushwood (hazel is by far the best) alongside and between the canes.

But a more fundamental problem is that, as the plants grow up the canes, they become bushier and more tangled. As they do this the canes are converging at the top of the wigwam, so as the plants take up more space there is less space available to support them. The result is that string must be wound round to keep all the growth in place.

Making a vertical cylinder of wire netting works better. At its simplest, a 2.4cm/8ft stake is knocked in to the ground and a 12.5cm/5in potful of seedlings is planted alongside. Next a 1.8m/6ft length of wire mesh about 90cm/3ft across is curled into a cylinder and secured with wire ties. The whole cylinder (about 30cm/12in in diameter) is set alongside the stake, around the newly planted seedlings, and stapled to the timber. The plants grow up the centre of the wire cylinder, then out to the wire curling their tendrils as they go, making an informal column of colour. This approach can be expanded by using two or three stakes and a larger piece of mesh to make a more substantial display with the plants set individually around the wire.

For a background to a border, to divide a vegetable plot, for masses of cut flowers or simply to create a hedge of colour, netting stretched between posts will do a fine job. Plastic netting 1.8m/6ft high can be secured with string or staples to 2.1–2.4m/7–8ft posts knocked 30–60cm/1–2ft into the ground 2.4m/8ft apart. Pea and bean netting with a 7.5–15cm/3–6in mesh is ideal. For a more solid and permanent job, use wire netting; again a wide mesh is suitable and this is sometimes sold as sheep or pig netting.

A simpler version of this, for a single upright feature in a border, is to set a 60–90cm/2–3ft wide sheet of steel netting 1.8m/6ft high vertically in the border stapled to two 2.4m/8ft timber posts. Pots of sweet peas, or individual plants, are set behind it and encouraged to grow up the mesh.

In all these cases prepare the ground for planting first, then put the supports in place and plant the sweet peas.

When planting under shrubs, the only support required is that which will help the stems reach the branches of the shrub; short lengths of twiggy brushwood are ideal. If tall brushwood is available, a ring of branches can be used as support instead of a ring of canes – it looks altogether more rustic and less stark. Lock the individual branches together by winding stout string around at two heights.

Various steel and woven hazel, willow or birch structures are also available as more elegant, and instant, support structures; make sure the design fits into the general style of your house and garden.

Shorter sweet peas require a different approach. Explorer and other Intermediate varieties can be allowed simply to grow into a tangled clump but support from 60–90cm/2–3ft brushwood is advisable. Dwarf varieties like Cupid, Pinocchio and Bijou can be grown without support.

Training

When sweet peas are grown naturally, as "bushes", the first aim is to encourage the shoots to climb rather than meander off across the garden. If they are grown on canes without additional netting, a little brushwood around the base will provide initial support or the shoots can be tied to the canes with soft twine.

As sweet peas grow, the shoot tips and tendrils move, searching for a support on which to cling. A little help is often advisable, and shoots and tendrils can be tucked behind mesh to help them grip. But be aware that these soft young growths are fragile so handle them carefully. As the plants grow, wayward shoots may need tucking in or tying in place, depending on the training method.

Dead-heading

Preventing the plants from setting seed ensures that they flower for as long as possible. Of course, if the flowers are picked regularly for cutting this will not be necessary but, should a holiday be taken during the flowering season, ask a neighbour to keep picking them so that flowers are still opening on your return.

If the plants are grown for display then dead-heading is essential. There is no short cut; flowers must be snipped off where they join the stem. Sometimes the fading flowers will drop off without setting seed; snip the bare stems off anyway.

12.5–15cm/5–6in flower pot alongside the plant; this can then be regularly filled and water will drain out through the drainage holes directly down to the roots without the risk of it running all over the border.

Large towers and wigwams and straight runs of netting are best watered with seephose, rubber hose with microperforations through which water steadily oozes. Lay it along the row, or around the tower or wigwam, before mulching, and when connected to the mains a slow steadily trickle of water soaks under the mulch and straight into the soil: exactly where it is needed. This approach wastes no water through evaporation or wind drift but supplies it direct to the roots where it is required.

Feeding

If preparation has been thorough, liquid feeding during the season should not be necessary. However, not all of us are able to prepare as carefully and comprehensively as we would wish and liquid feeding during the season can improve health and prolong flowering. A low-nitrogen liquid feed is ideal, and should be applied generously to ensure it reaches down to the full root depth. Depending on the inherent fertility of the soil, weekly or two-weekly applications should be sufficient. Specific sweet pea feeds have been available periodically over the years, either for raking in as dry feeds or for diluting in water; use these when they are available.

Water

Sweet peas love water – as long as the soil is sufficiently well drained to avoid waterlogging. This prolongs flowering, increases the number of flowers per stem, ensures individual flowers last as long as possible and generally improves health. Leaving a slight depression allows water from a can or hosepipe to be poured on and kept in the required area.

An alternative for clumps of sweet peas grown into shrubs or trained on narrow supports is to sink a

Growing on cordons

This method, used primarily by serious exhibitors and, to a lesser extent, by gardeners wanting high-quality cut flowers, depends on restricting the growth of each plant to a single shoot, which results in larger flowers on very much longer stems. The fact that the plants also have more light and are less tangled also improves the placement of the individual flowers. Experienced individual exhibitors have developed their own, more

Young cordons growing well with the first flowers beginning to open.

Stems are tied in individually with rings, twine or, in this case, plastic tape.

sophisticated variants of these techniques; here I give only a basic outline.

Autumn sowing is almost essential: the more extensive root growth that this allows is an important factor in the increased vigour of the plants; sowing in late winter is a useful alternative, but leaving it until spring does not allow the plants sufficient time for root development before flowering.

Supports can be put in place during the winter, after the trench has been prepared. First, erect a stout vertical post at each end of the row; a 2.4m/8ft, 10cm x 10cm/4in x 4in post sunk 60cm/2ft into the ground is ideal. Next fix a 2ft/60cm-long piece, 10cm x 5cm/4in x 2in, across the top of each post on the outer end. Now run a length of galvanized wire from both ends of the crosspiece to their counterparts at the other end of the row and tighten. This wire will support canes to which individual plants are trained. Next insert a 2.4m/8ft bamboo cane vertically every 20–23cm/8–9in along each side and tie the top to the wire with twine. This will give you a double row of vertical canes, securely supported.

In spring, usually in March or early April, plant one plant alongside each cane, about 5cm/2in to the side. Water in with liquid feed. After planting, all but one of the shoots should be removed from each plant but do not do this immediately; the energy produced by the foliage on three or four shoots is invaluable. In late April or early May, snip off all the shoots but one. Do not necessarily choose to

A row of mature flowering cordons showing the vertical canes, tied in securely with wire.

keep the tallest: the most robust is usually more suitable, even if shorter. Tie in the remaining shoot, which should be 23–30cm/9–12in high, using twine, wire rings, sweet pea support clips or using a taping machine. As the shoots grow, tie in again so that they never swing to the side or bend over. A tie at every leaf joint is ideal.

Soon, side shoots will start to appear on your chosen shoot; these should be snipped off, and tendrils too should be removed so that only the main shoot and its foliage remains tied to the cane. Flowers will start to appear when the plants are about 60–90cm/2–3ft high; the early flowers will not be top-quality blooms but can be cut for the house; do not leave them on the plants.

Adequate watering is essential; I find seephose run along each side at the base of the canes works well but it's important not to overdo it or the roots may start to rot and the whole plant decline. The first quality flowers should be produced in May; the stems should continue to be tied in, disbudded and the tendrils removed regularly.

Clearly, as the plants approach the tops of their canes, something has to be done to accommodate the burgeoning growth. In essence, the plants are untied from their canes, the stems laid on the ground along the row for a distance of 60cm/2ft, then the plants tied in again to a new cane and guided up it. This must be done in a careful and organized manner, avoiding stepping on the shoots; you will also need some extra canes across the ends of the row at this stage. Having done this, the stems now have extra cane height in which to grow and flower.

Experienced growers and the specialist societies will be able to advise on the far greater degree of detail which must be considered when growing for exhibition; the foregoing will nonetheless provide an idea of the general process.

Quick guide to looking after sweet peas

1. Choose a sunny place.
2. Fork over soil and rake in a handful of general fertilizer to the square yard.
3. Put in wire, brushwood or cane supports before planting.
4. Sow two seeds every 6in/25cm in spring OR plant individual plants 6in/15cm apart OR plant a potful of plants in a clump.
5. Water in with liquid feed.
6. Guide any wayward stems so they climb in the right direction.
7. Watch for greenfly and spray if necessary.
8. Dead-head as the flowers fade or cut regularly for the house.
9. Drench thoroughly in dry spells.

Chapter Eleven
Creating new sweet peas

Creating your very own new sweet pea is one of the most exciting achievements for any sweet pea enthusiast. Many home gardeners have raised sweet peas which have gone on to become very popular and while seed companies and professional plant breeders are also continually creating and introducing new varieties, home gardeners have an opportunity to make a valuable contribution.

And it can be worthwhile in a financial sense as well as in terms of personal satisfaction. The retail flower seed companies will pay for the rights to sell the best of the new varieties in their catalogues and the very fact that your new variety is being made widely available, and may even appear on the racks of your local garden centre, is in itself a source of satisfaction. But varieties which achieve such a level of success are few and usually produced by experienced sweet pea breeders – who do not need me to tell them how to go about it.

For newcomers, the following should be kept in mind. Start with a clear idea of what you want to achieve. For example, if you have noticed some deficiency in varieties of a particular shade, then focus on improving that feature. Be aware, though, that in the traditional Spencer types, there are few breakthroughs remaining to be made by the home breeder. The intensity of some colours can probably be enhanced; giving the blues the range of shades we already have in the pinks is a possibility (especially picotees); there is surely more to come in bicoloured combinations and 'reverse' bicolours; and reverse picotees, with a white edge to a dark flower or a blue edge to a pink one; veined, as distinct from flaked types, known as Marbles, are almost undeveloped. And, should they take your fancy, so called duplex or 'double' flower forms where a second, or even a third, standard sits in front of the first may appeal; there have been varieties of this sort in the past, but no longer.

It is interesting that, from the exhibitor's point of view, increasing the number of flowers on the stem is frowned upon: "I am quite sure that we encounter another very real risk in seeking to increase the number of flowers on a stem," wrote Charles W. J. Unwin in 1986. Why? If you are an exhibitor, then the even placement of flowers on a stem is paramount and ensuring that five or six flowers are all fresh and at their best at the same time *and* placed perfectly is almost impossible. But in the garden... who cares? In general, the more flowers the better, hence the development of Multifloras and so-called Super Multifloras for the garden; another useful direction for the home breeder.

On the way to a good yellow, this rich and creamy yellow-centred form is a result of bringing together blood from L. belinensis and a traditional Spencer sweet pea.

Almost all the material written about sweet pea breeding relates to breeding with exhibition in mind. If that is your aim, fine. But this is a book more with gardeners in mind than exhibitors and the features which exhibitors consider make a good variety are less important than those which make a good garden variety.

However, in the garden, flowers are often seen from three or even all sides; it is therefore helpful if individual blooms, and even spikes, have more than one "face". So a flower which tends to hold its wings horizontally will have less impact in the garden than one which tends to hold its wings angled down on either side of the keel. (In the same way, modern Siberian irises with their horizontal falls have less impact than older varieties whose falls hang down.) A flower with flat wings looks colourful when looking directly towards the standard as the colour in the standard is in full view. But look from the side, as will inevitably happen with plants grown on towers or wigwams, and the edge of the standard shows very little colour; but if the wings are angled down around the keel then the face of one wing will be in full view from whichever side the flower is viewed.

Another way the demands of the gardener vary from those of the exhibitor is in the placement of the flowers on the stem. The exhibitor requires the flowers to face in one direction when grown on cordons, to stand in one plane. In the garden, if flowers are held all round the stem, facing in all directions, then colour is visible from every angle. This has been achieved in foxgloves, for example, in which the wild *Digitalis purpurea* carries its flowers only on one side of the spikes while in 'Excelsior' and 'Foxy' the flowers are distributed all round the stem creating a more colourful effect. Clearly, there is a difference between flowers like foxgloves which are held above the foliage in a spike and those of sweet peas which tend to be held alongside the foliage; the flowers naturally turn away from the shade of the remainder of the plant and towards the light. But the point is that where garden display is the primary use, a fixation with flowers which are held in a single plane on one side of the stem is unnecessary.

Another factor which would enhance the effect of the sweet pea in the garden is if two flower stems rather than just one were to be produced at a single leaf joint. Even a tendency in this direction would improve the garden display, although on any but an otherwise naturally vigorous plant this might result in stems which were uncomfortably short for cutting even if the garden enjoyment was increased.

Yellow flowers, of course, have been a target for sweet pea breeders for decades but it has already been shown that conventional plant breeding techniques are unlikely to bring about such a revolutionary shade; this is a job for professionals with access to laboratory techniques and even then the genetic incompatibilities are far from solved.

Bernard Jones and other British breeders, in a group under the auspices of the NSPS, worked for some years to try to create a yellow sweet pea by crossing white Spencers with wild species – but it came to nothing. Now Dr Keith Hammett, using the recently discovered *L. belinensis* as a parent and embryo rescue techniques to ensure the survival of resulting seedlings, has made significant progress towards good yellows and also, from the same parentage, created some sparkling blues and bicolours. However, at the time of writing, he is still working on adding the familiar necessary qualities of contemporary Spencers or Modern Grandifloras to these new colours.

Increasing the vase life by breeding is also, perhaps, beyond the scope of the home breeder purely because of the requirement for facilities to allow comprehensive testing, but it would surely bring benefits to home gardeners, commercial growers and buyers of cut flowers.

Working with dwarf types is becoming more popular: with no staking to be done, they take less time to look after. And from a commercial point of view there is a definite upturn in demand, as the numbers of recent introductions in this group show. It is perhaps important to be aware that there have, in the past, been false dawns for dwarf sweet peas and it may well happen again. Clearly, however, breeding dwarf sweet peas is not for gardeners with back problems but it does take less work, and less space than breeding climbing varieties.

This sparkling red and blue bicolour is a surprising descendant of L. belinensis and Spencer sweet peas.

and colour combinations, combined with the fragrance which is always in demand in this group, would be well worth pursuing.

It is important for the home breeder with limited resources of time and space to be very selective by choosing two projects, or perhaps just one, upon which to concentrate and not be diverted by other fancies. A diffusion of energies among different projects will result in too few seedlings being grown to allow the full range of genetic combinations to be revealed, resulting in less progress than if fewer targets were selected.

And this brings me to another point. It is important to grow as many seedlings as possible to assess the full range of diversity resulting from any one cross – and it is also crucial to throw almost all of them away. Throwing away the slightly substandard is as important as selecting the choice. For, as they say, it is impossible not to love one's own children – but when raising sweet peas it is *essential* to be hard-hearted and select only the very best for future development. You need a ruthless streak to breed good sweet peas.

Crossing technique

Sweet peas are both naturally self-pollinating and naturally self-fertile, meaning that if you do nothing, the pollen in a sweet pea flower will pollinate that same flower and seed will result. Bees and other insects do not pollinate sweet peas although, on rare occasions, when leaf cutter bees split the keel and expose the stigma, or when excessive drought causes petals and keel to wilt with the same result, cross-pollination may occur. In order to cross two different varieties the gardener must take a hand. You will need a pair of tweezers and a pair of short nail scissors.

First of all, choose a spike or two from the plant you wish to be the pollen parent and cut them from the plant. Choose spikes with at least one recently opened flower in which the pollen will be fresh.

Next, choose a flower spike on the plant you wish to carry the seed; the bottom flower should be in bud but just about to open. Lift the standard out of the way, and pull the two wings apart to allow access to the keel – which contains the male and

Bringing the colours, colour combinations and flower quality of the Spencers into dwarf types suitable for patio containers is a very practical objective, together with increasing the flower size and the number of flowers on each stem, so increasing the flowering intensity; enhancing the mostly modest fragrance would also be welcome. Increasing the stem length of the dwarf types could also be attempted – not so much to create patio varieties which will double as sources of cut flowers (although this is doubtless an eminently marketable concept) but to create cut-flower varieties which can be easily grown without the necessity for support or training.

The other area of current interest, and demand, is for new Grandifloras where new colours female parts of the flower. Parting the two halves of the keel will reveal the sexual organs.

Examine the ten anthers to be sure that they have shed absolutely no pollen; if the pollen on the anthers is dry and powdery it is too late to use the flower as a seed parent; the flower may already have been pollinated by its own pollen and a second pollination will be futile. If this is the case, choose another flower.

If the pollen is still held in the anthers on the potential seed parent, use the scissors to snip along the top of the keel or vertically down the sides, to allow access to the anthers, then carefully remove them with the tweezers.

Expose the anthers of the pollen parent with their pollen and dust this pollen on to the stigma of the seed parent. This can also be done by removing the pollen with a sable paint brush and using it to transfer the pollen to the stigma. Midday on a humid day is supposedly the best time for pollinating, but for most gardeners the best time is 'when you have time'.

Label the stem that will carry the seed at once. Different breeders use different systems of labelling. You can use a standard white plastic plant label, date it, write the cross in full, with the seed parent first as is usual, for example 'Rosy Frills' x 'Albutt Blue'. Tie it to the stem with soft twine; this then becomes the label for the seed pot. Alternatively, you can tie a piece of coloured wool on the stem as a marker, or use a tie-on paper tag which can be numbered, and make a note of the cross in a notebook. The details of the cross can be noted on a soft tie-on plastic label and then transferred to a more permanent label for sowing.

Having made your cross, you can pinch off the remaining flowers but you may well find that two flowers on a stem are both receptive; pollinate these as well. Alternatively, pollinate additional flowers elsewhere on the same plant and label them all individually. There is no need to cover your pollinated flower with a muslin bag to keep bees from pollinating your flowers as is sometimes suggested – though a bag can be useful in collecting seed should you be away when the seed is ready later in summer.

At this stage relatively few seeds, and therefore few pollinations, are required, as it is usual for all the offspring of this first cross, known as the F1 generation, to be identical. For breeding purposes, you are going to be more interested in the generation that follows, rather than this one.

Keep the plant which is to be the seed parent healthy, well fed and well watered and wait for the pods to swell and start to dry off. When the pod has become brown and dry, and the seeds start to rattle, remove the pod and the label and put both in a brown paper bag or an old envelope, ready to catch the seed; take great care when actually removing the pod from the plant as, if the pods are left a little too long, the initial disturbance can be enough to pop the pod and seed will fly out. The slightest further delay could result in this happening spontaneously.

The next two years

Sow your precious seed in October or November in a 12.5cm/5in pot in the usual way and plant out in a clump, not on cordons. When they flower, the flowers of all seedlings should look the same, though not necessarily like either parent.

In this first year you have to do exactly nothing, except look after the plants and ensure they thrive healthily. The plants will naturally pollinate themselves without your assistance. Then as the seed ripens, collect it, ensure that it is labelled and keep it for sowing in the autumn. By contrast with the seed collected from the initial pollination, when relatively little is required, at this stage it pays to collect and sow as many seeds as you can reasonably fit into your space and can look after in the time you have available: it is at this stage that the variation appears, and the more plants are grown, the more variation will be generated, and the better the chance of something special being revealed.

Seed of this second generation can be sown in 12.5cm/5in pots as before, but when planting out it pays to separate the plants and set them individually along wire. It is important to be able easily to distinguish between one plant and the next (and many may be very similar), in order to be sure that when you select an individual, there is no confusion with its neighbour. This second generation, the result of allowing the F1 generation to self-pollinate, is called the F2 generation.

The variability at this stage can be surprising and it is important to keep in mind your aim in making the cross in the first place. Make a very small selection that best fits your criteria, at the same time not automatically rejecting absolutely everything else; something surprising, new and distinct may well arise which should also be retained. But be fairly ruthless. It is easy to be tempted to keep too many.

Carefully label each of those which are to be retained, and ensure that they thrive healthily, then collect seed separately from each at the end of the season. It is wise to remove unwanted plants on either side of any from which you intend to collect seed to avoid any possible chance of contamination, either by freak cross-pollination or by inadvertently collecting seed from the wrong plant.

I repeat that at this stage it is easy to choose too many plants which look good. Very many of the seedlings will be beautiful but it is crucial to be sure that seedlings are selected which are distinct from existing varieties; there is no point going through this whole process only to end up with a variety which is indistinguishable from one which is already being grown. If it is exactly the same colour, it may still be an improvement through having a stronger stem, better scent or being more prolific; but do not be tempted to save too many – there will be insufficient space to grow them all. The more seeds from each plant which can be grown, again individually on one wire, the better.

Make sure the seedlings from the different plants are labelled so their origin is clear. As they flower, the F3 generation, it will become more obvious if your selected seedlings are 'coming true': that is, if all the progeny are identical both to each other and to their parent if left to self-pollinate in the usual way. This is your goal. If the progeny are not identical, save seed from those that are, grow the seed from each plant separately and continue in this way, discarding off-types. Some, it has to be said, will never come true and must be rejected.

Be sure to consider not only colour, but other less immediately noticeable characteristics: flowering period, scent, flower form, stem length, number of flowers per stem, number of seeds produced per pod and the number of flowers which fail to set seed

at all. It is easy to ignore the capacity for setting seed generously, but this is a feature upon which the commercial potential of an otherwise promising new seedling could fail.

Some of your selections may never produce a constant crop of seedlings; they may repeatedly break down and so have to be abandoned. Others may take a few years to develop a pure stock. Once a whole batch of seedlings grown from the seed of a single plant is identical, then it is likely that the variety is already fixed. If this is not the case, repeat the process of growing on the progeny of individual plants and again assess the results. In this generation you may well find a true batch.

It is interesting that in his book, *Sweet Peas*, published back in 1953, no less than E. R. Janes states: "I cannot help thinking that trueness has largely been overstressed, and that most keen growers would not object to a small percentage of untrue plants if they knew what to expect." This is not a popular view, to put it kindly, as the periodic criticism of rogues in Wisley trials, over many decades, indicates.

Choosing parents

The first criterion for good parents is that they themselves must be fixed and true-breeding with no tendency to produce rogues. If you start with one parent (or worse, two) which is not fixed then this characteristic will be transferred to the progeny.

The result from making a cross will be the same whichever parent is used to carry the seed, but if one is known to be relatively unproductive it is clearly more sensible to use the other for this purpose.

An objective usually starts with an idea of varying or improving an existing variety – you might think: "I'd like to create a blue version of 'Rosy Frills'," with its broad pink picotee. 'Rosy Frills' is clearly going to be one parent and, as the other, you might choose an excellent dark blue like 'Oxford Blue', which has a good scent. It might also be worth trying an existing picotee like 'Albutt Blue', which has only a very narrow blue edge, or even a blue picotee Grandiflora type like 'Romeo'.

It is not important to grow many plants of the F1 generation, but in the F2 generation you must grow a great many plants – at least 100 seedlings of each cross, and preferably two or three times as many. And, even so, you may not get a blue 'Rosy Frills', which also has a good Spencer flower form or an elegant and pure Grandiflora form. There are, it has to be said, genetic reasons why this might not work at all, but surely it is worth a try.

Another interesting project, and perhaps more realistic, would be to introduce flake characteristic into Intermediate types, although some work has already been done in this area. For Intermediate flakes choose a good flake such as the recently introduced scarlet 'Oklahoma' and as the other parent a Jet Set, Continental or Cupid/Sweetie type. We know that the flake feature is controlled by two genes so it is important to grow even more seedlings in the F2 generation than was necessary for the blue 'Rosy Frills' – again, it is clear why it is important not to make too many crosses.

An altogether more realistic project might be to create a Intermediate version of the wonderful dark stripe 'Nimbus' – and, from the home gardener's point of view, working with shorter types is a lot less work. The genetics tell us that crossing a Jet Set, or a Continental type, on to 'Nimbus' would give a one in 64 chance of producing exactly the desired result, so grow about 200 in the F2 generation, just to be sure.

When you think you have something really good

There are two traditional routes to take with new seedlings. There are classes at shows for new and unnamed seedlings and if you feel your variety has show potential then show it. However, for selections with more garden potential than show value, trials are a better route. In the British trials at Wisley in Surrey, at Harlow Carr in Yorkshire and at Glasgow, newcomers are assessed for their garden performance and awards given accordingly. Note that British trials will accept entries from overseas.

But before going to this trouble it will surely be worth showing your newcomer to other sweet pea enthusiasts: they may, after all, reveal how similar it is to another variety with which you may be

unfamiliar. Or they may enthuse so much at what a breakthrough it is and suggest *not* sending it to trial for fear it would be pirated – someone may just come along in the autumn and collect seed from the trials for their own use; trials are conducted in public gardens, after all.

The retailers of sweet pea seed all hold their own private trials and you may consider it worthwhile to submit your variety to one, or a number, of them. Make contact first, then send a photograph and detailed description. If they prove interested, insist on a "test and talk" agreement in which you give them the right to grow and assess your variety but not to market it or breed from it without a further agreement.

In spite of over 200 years of development, there is still plenty of potential in the sweet pea; the only constraints are our imagination, the genetics of the plant, and the time and space to grow enough seedlings. It is true that professional plant breeders, with their laboratory facilities and their staff growing many thousands of seedlings a year, are more likely to create dramatic breakthroughs; but home gardeners can still come up with new and beautiful flowers.

Walter W. Wright, in his endearingly eccentric *A Book About Sweet Peas*, published in 1910, has some good advice: "What can be done to prevent the country from being flooded with sorts that are only dissimilar in name from existing varieties? Two things, and I earnestly beg every raiser of Sweet Peas to practise them. In the first place, let him grow his novelty for at least three years before he makes any attempt to dispose of (i.e. sell) it. While he has it in his garden let him 'rogue' it rigorously... The raiser's second step is to make himself a member of the special society which exists for the developing of the Sweet Pea, because one of the duties which this excellent body sets itself is the examination and trial of novelties."

Anyone interested in breeding sweet peas should join the National Sweet Pea Society. The society's *Annual*, in particular, regularly features reports, histories, personal accounts and advice on techniques from home breeders. Awareness of the experiences of others can help new breeders avoid mistakes.

Chapter Twelve
Solving sweet pea problems

Grow any plants together in large quantities and they will be attacked by pests, diseases and other maladies – the exhibitor growing rows of plants alongside one another is more likely to see problems on his plants than the gardener growing a few plants under more natural conditions in different places around the garden. Some widespread pests and diseases attack sweet peas, and they also have their own special problems but, fortunately, they are not especially prone to incurable maladies. This is a fairly comprehensive list of problems, and may look alarming; however, most are uncommon.

Anthracnose

This fungus disease is not known in Britain but has been found on sweet peas in the warmer, southern states of the USA. Young shoots are brittle, and shoots, leaves and flowers are marked with small white spots, on the young growth at first but spreading down the plant; wilting follows, then death. There is no treatment.

Aphids

These familiar sap-sucking insects cause weak growth but they also transmit virus diseases so are the most significant sweet pea problem. The pea aphid, a relatively large creature which comes in yellow, pale green and pink colour, is one of the main species but some others are also troublesome.

The few remaining systemic insecticides on the market will do a good job controlling them, as will the many less toxic contact insecticides, but as their name implies, these must come into actual contact with the insect to kill it so careful and thorough spraying is necessary. Insecticidal soaps and other non-toxic alternatives are also effective but, again, success depends on careful application.

Blindness

This is a physiological problem, rather than a disease, in which a previously healthy-looking plant will begin to look slightly crumpled, then its shoots stop growing. The best remedy is simply to pull it up.

Botrytis

More common in badly grown glasshouse cut-flower crops than in the garden, but in damp summers botrytis can cause white flower spotting, especially in blue varieties, and brown spots on white-flowered varieties. It also attacks as a grey mould elsewhere on the plant. Effective chemicals for the home gardener are few, and the arrival of hot, dry and sunny weather is most likely to prompt an improvement in the situation.

Bud drop

A perplexing problem causing the individual buds on a stem to fail to develop fully and then drop off before they open. Disastrous for the exhibitor, and infuriating for the gardener, this seems to be caused, not by a disease organism, but rather it follows, sometimes a week or two later, sudden cold weather, perhaps combined with drying winds. Poor light conditions are also a factor, along with nitrogen-rich soil. Extreme drought is a more obvious cause of the problem, but at least this is one which can be solved by keeping roots constantly moist.

It seems that some varieties are more prone to bud drop than others but the effect on a given variety can vary in different seasons and on different soils.

Crown gall

A bacterial infection, usually splashed from the soil on to small wounds in the stem; the result is irregular swelling at around ground level. Usually more alarming than harmful, which is just as well as there is no cure.

Leaf scorch

Perhaps most common on cordons on light, sandy soil, but still unusual. The colour fades from the lower leaves but at first the plants keep growing fairly well. As the problem proceeds up the plant growth inevitably slows and the plant becomes useless. Said to be more common in scarlet and orange varieties. Light shading and adding organic matter to the soil will help.

Leafy gall

A bacterial problem in which clusters of unnaturally short, thickened and distorted shoots develop, often on the lower parts of the plant. It is also possible that leafy gall is a contributory factor in blindness.

This uncommon disease is caused by an organism which is usually found in the soil; it is uncertain quite how it infects the plants. Sweet peas should not be grown again on the site on which this problem is seen. The disease can also be transmitted by seed, so do not save seed from infected plants.

Leatherjackets

These larvae of the crane fly (known in Britain as daddy-long-legs) can occasionally be very damaging to direct-sown seedlings in the open garden – one reason, perhaps, that when direct sowing was

far more common the sowing rate was very high to allow the leatherjackets a few meals without ruining the final display. Usually only troublesome when a lawn is dug up or turves used in trenches.

Mice

Devastating to seed pots, mice can dig up and eat all your seeds in one night. In frames, make sure the lids fit tightly and set traps among the seed pots. If traditional traps are used, rather than live traps, be sure to set each under a 12.5cm/5in flower pot raised on stones (or in a long length of drainpipe) to prevent birds being caught accidentally.

The danger is not over once seeds have germinated, as the young shoots merely serve as markers for the seed below, which can be swiftly excavated and devoured.

Once planted in the garden, plants are unlikely to be damaged although mice will very occasionally nibble shoots. Seeds sown direct are especially vulnerable, and again, traps should be set. It also pays to store your seed where mice cannot have access.

Mildew (downy)

Unlike powdery mildew, with which it is sometimes confused, downy mildew is relatively uncommon and is exacerbated by cool, damp conditions. Yellow patches become visible on the upper surfaces of the leaves while, underneath the patches, a purple-tinted, white mould appears. Eventually the infected areas turn brown and die.

Fungicides are available which control this disease but cultural control is more difficult. Although the same species of mildew also attacks broad beans and peas, each host has its own specific race of mildew and cross-infection does not take place.

Mildew (powdery)

Probably the most common fungus disease of sweet peas, small greyish white spots or patches appear on the leaves and then coalesce and spread to more of the plant; the leaves may begin to turn yellow and in severe cases will then drop off.

A pollen beetle nestles among flower petals.

Powdery mildew is the most widespread and destructive of sweet pea diseases.

Powdery mildew is generally most troublesome in hot, dry spells with low humidity; keeping plants well watered in these conditions helps reduce the impact. Many fungicides, both organic and non-organic, are available to control the problem but in long, dry spells repeated application may be necessary.

Although not infected by the species of powdery mildew found on roses, the mildew which attacks lupins and culinary peas can also attack sweet peas. This should be considered while planning cropping.

Mosaic (see Virus)

Pea weevil

The very distinctive damage of this irritating pest is a series of neat notches eaten out of the edges of leaves by the adults. More common on culinary peas, and especially clover, seedlings can be set back in spring when the adults emerge from hibernation and feed on foliage, their young feeding on the root nodules later in spring. By the time these too hatch later in summer, sweet peas are unlikely to be a target – younger, juicer material will be preferred. Some insecticides will kill the adults.

Seed exported from Britain into the United States is often fumigated to kill this pest but it is thought this treatment may reduce germination.

Pollen beetle

Small black beetles are found on the flowers, especially in the keel. They are more unsightly than damaging (page 124). The problem can be minimized by standing yellow buckets half full of water near the rows; the beetles are attracted by the yellow colouring and drown in the water.

Root and foot rot

The "foot" of the plant is not the root, but the point at which the stem joins the root. Fungus infection can move up to this point from the root or from the foot downwards into the root system. The familiar damping-off disease, usually of less robust seedlings, is one type of foot rot and in sweet peas the damage usually takes place when the plants are small – they stop growing and then fade away; black lesions may be seen on what remains of the roots. Occasionally more mature plants are affected and it can be tempting to ascribe this to some vague inadequacy in a particular seedling. However, the roots will be found to have a black discoloration and if this occurs more than occasionally consider moving the sweet peas to another part of the garden.

Often caused by *Pythium* and *Phytophthera* fungi, but also other species including *Thievaliopsis*, these organisms are usually present in the soil all the time and attack plants when under stress from another cause. The damage can occur in seed pots or in the open ground, and is especially likely when the soil or compost is over-rich in nitrogen and so excessive use of fertilizer or manure should be avoided.

It is also important never to water seedlings in pots with water from rain barrels, which are notorious reservoirs of infection: there is little point in sowing seed in sterile compost and then introducing disease with the water.

Root nodules

It can be a worry to novice sweet pea growers, planting out or removing their plants in the autumn, to notice small lumps all over the roots of their sweet peas; an infection is suspected. Be assured that these root nodules are an integral part of plants in the pea

family and contain bacteria which assimilate nitrogen from the air in the soil and make it available to the plant. Sweet peas are legumes and 'nitrogen fixing' is an essential feature of them all.

Sclerotinia

An uncommon infection, known as cottonyrot in the USA, and most prevalent in damp areas. It attacks the plant at the base of the stem, at a leaf joint or between leaflets where fluffy white mould is seen – usually associated with, or followed by, the wilting of the plant. Carefully dig up and burn infected plants and move the sweet pea bed to another part of the garden for at least three years.

Seed rotting

Seeds rot in their pods before germinating. Not to be confused with germination failure caused by a hard seed coat failing to admit moisture. Usually caused by one of the damping-off fungi, especially *Pythium*, and exacerbated in varieties with very soft seed coats or in poorly produced seed; seedlings simply fail to appear as a result of the seed rotting.

Do not over-firm seed compost when filling pots, avoid overwatering of seed pots and never water them with water from a rain barrel.

Slugs can damage mature foliage as well as eat young seedlings.

Slugs and snails

Slugs and snails, familiar pests to most gardeners, can be troublesome in two ways. They can attack seedlings in pots or in the open and nibble off shoots before they have an opportunity to develop. They can also graze on the lower foliage of more mature plants, causing the leaves to look unsightly and vigour to be reduced. Organic or chemical controls, traps and biological controls are all effective.

Streak

In the original use of the term, this referred to a now-uncommon disease which caused reddish or brownish streaks on stems and leaves. The term is now sometimes used loosely to describe yellow or reddish streaks on any part of the plant, caused by a range of maladies – and even to describe virus infection and flower breaking.

Thrips

Sometimes known as thunderflies or thunderbugs, these small, slender insects, just a few millimetres long, are important pests not only because they cause mottling and silvering of young foliage and shoot tips but also because they transmit tomato spotted wilt virus. Chemical control is not difficult: spray at the first sign of damage.

Virus

Virus diseases are the most serious problems for enthusiastic sweet pea growers. The current count, according to the Royal Horticultural Society, is 11 different viruses which infect sweet peas although only five are really significant. These are either known by colloquial names like "streak" or "mosaic" or by more formal names such as pea enation mosaic virus.

Plants are infected when aphids or thrips feed on already infected plants, often related plants like clover or culinary peas, but also weeds and other unrelated hosts, then move to the sweet peas where the virus is transferred as the insects feed on sap. So keeping plants free of aphids and thrips must be the preventative, together with keeping control of weeds and ensuring that other plants in the garden are pest-free. Once a plant has developed the disease, it cannot be controlled; plants should be pulled up and burned. Virus does not persist in the soil but there is some evidence that it can be carried in seed. Some can also be carried on secateurs and spread from one plant to another while dead-heading and removing side shoots.

The five main viruses which affect sweet peas are:

Pea enation mosaic virus Characteristic translucent "windows" appear in leaves, and sometimes flowers, usually from mid-season onwards; sometimes the leaves are also puckered. Distortion of the top of the plant, sometimes known as fuzzyhead, is common and flowers show colour breaking (streaks of a different colour) especially in red- and blue-flowered varieties. Transmitted by the pea aphid which brings infection from clover in particular, but also other members of the pea family. Clearly it pays to keep lawn clover under control. The incidence varies from year to year.

This virus has a number of interesting features. Firstly, it is only present in the infecting aphid for a short time, so unless preventative spraying is practised, and this is now greatly discouraged, spraying is often ineffective. This virus is also spread on knives and secateurs and is likely to be seed-borne.

Bean yellow mosaic virus Veins in the youngest leaves become clear or translucent followed by mottling and brown streaks on the leaf stalks and stem. Sometimes there is flower-breaking. This virus is also aphid-transmitted and, like pea enation mosaic virus, is not persistent in its carrier. Several strains of this virus exist, not all infecting all theoretical host plants.

Pea mosaic virus Perhaps the most common sweet pea virus, infection shows as mottling and yellowing of the leaves which will have both dark green and yellow, often slightly sunken, patches as well as flower-breaking. Transmitted by aphids from many host plants in the pea family.

White clover mosaic virus Causes weak growth, distortion of flowers and leaf mottling – any stunted plants should be immediately removed. Symptoms are most obvious in cool seasons.

The streaks in the flowers are the result of virus infection; behind are healthy white flowers from the same variety.

Its method of transmission is not yet fully understood but it can be spread by handling and on secateurs.

Tomato spotted wilt virus Had become less common in Britain in recent years though still infecting begonias, dahlias (when it is known as dahlia ringspot virus) and zantedeschias as well as, occasionally, sweet peas. Until recently it has been more common in the United States where it has a wide host range, including grasses, and causes reddish-brown streaks on the stems and characteristic yellow circular spots on the leaves which turn brown. Spread by thrips, so these and garden weeds should be controlled.

In recent years, with the rapid spread of western flower thrips in commercial glasshouses, tomato spotted wilt virus has again become more widespread but as this particular thrip is uncommon out of doors in Britain (though an effective vector in warmer areas of the US), infection of sweet peas is largely restricted to cut-flower crops grown under glass.

White mould

This relatively uncommon disease, sometimes known as ramularia leaf spot, can be confused with powdery mildew but tends to be prevalent in cool, damp conditions rather than in hot, dry spells. Symptoms vary: look for a white mildew-like covering on leaves and stems and water-soaked spots without definite margins; the infected parts of the plant, usually the lower leaves at first, become yellow, usually starting at the base, then the leaves drop off.

Overhead watering can create a damp atmosphere which encourages the disease, especially in bush-grown plants, and it can also be spread by watersplash.

This is specific to sweet peas, so cannot spread from other plants, and is spread from year to year on old plants left standing, unrotted plants on compost heaps and so on. Not an easy disease to deal with by spraying as many of the effective chemicals have been removed from the market and those which remain may soon also vanish. Once an attack has occurred, grow sweet peas elsewhere for a year or two and be scrupulous about destroying old plants in the autumn.

Wilt

This disease, usually caused by *Verticillium* or *Fusarium* fungi, blocks the xylem (the channels which take sap up into the plant) and the result, as the name implies, is wilting of the plant. This may not be dramatic at first, and the plant may seem to recover overnight only to wilt again in the heat of the day; occasionally, and rather strangely, the effect may only be seen on one side of the plant – at least at first. Sometimes the effect is seen quite suddenly on a hot day at peak season – much like the sudden collapse of clematis attacked by its own wilt.

The symptoms can be similar to those caused by foot rot, but when the plant is dug up and destroyed (as it must be), cut cleanly through the stem 60–90cm/2–3ft above ground level; if wilt is the culprit a brown staining will be evident in the cut surface.

Chapter Thirteen
In the house

Sweet peas seem to end up in a vase more than almost any other flower; they invite themselves into your house like a disarmingly cute kitten. But I'm not going to advise you on how to arrange your sweet peas. Neither am I going to assume, as many books on sweet peas have in the past, that your aim is competitive flower-arranging at shows. After all, just a few flowers, on short stems, look delightful in a small vase on a desk, on a side table or as part of an individual place setting at a dinner party. And, of course, long-stemmed, cordon-grown flowers can be very impressive in larger, more elaborate arrangements with other material.

In smaller arrangements a couple of sweet pea shoots, with tendrils, look pretty as an accompaniment, and it has been traditional for larger displays to be finished with sweet pea foliage around the base. And I've noticed that some flowers look especially good with sweet peas, and these are my suggestions:

Acacia baileyana
> (feathery, silvery green-leaved mimosa)

Acacia baileyana 'Purpurea'
> (dusky purple-leaved mimosa)

Acacia dealbata
> (silver-leaved mimosa)

Asparagus densiflorus 'Sprengeri'
> (the familiar asparagus fern)

Begonia rex
> (many varieties with dark, prettily patterned foliage)

Cotinus coggygria 'Royal Purple'
> (sumptuous purple foliage)

Elymus magellanicus
> (silvery blue-leaved grass)

Gypsophila 'Covent Garden', 'Monarch White'
> (annual, white – though I find these last less well than perennial varieties)

Gypsophila 'Festival Pink', 'Flamingo'
> (perennial, pink)

Gypsophila 'White Festival', 'Bristol Fairy' and 'Schneeflocke'
> (perennial, double white)

Pennisetum setaceum 'Rubrum'
> (dark reddish foliage and plumes)

Salvia farinacea 'Cirrus'
> (white on silvered stems, slender spikes)

Salvia farinacea 'Strata'
> (blue and white bicolour, slender spikes)

Salvia farinacea 'Victoria'
> (dusky blue, slender spikes)

Saxifraga umbrosa
> (London's Pride, pretty rounded leaves)

Tanacetum niveum 'Jackpot'
> (dainty white daisies)

When arranging sweet peas on their own or with just a little foliage, some colours look better together than others. Pink and lavender is the traditional combination. Mauve and salmon-pink also works well. Pale blue and cream, dark blue and cream, maroon and cream, white with almost any other colour – all look good. Choosing different shades of the same colour together is also very pretty.

Cutting the flowers

If you need especially long-stemmed flowers for large arrangements then grow them on the cordon system, as exhibitors do, otherwise you may find the stems irritatingly short. In the descriptions you will find mention of those I know to be dependably long-stemmed. Try to cut your sweet peas first thing in the morning before the summer sun has begun to suck moisture from flowers and foliage. Cut the stems as long as you can, with just the first flower at the base of the spike fully open, and plunge them in cool water at once; take a bucket or other container with you to the garden rather than carry them round in the sun while you cut all you need.

I always use sharp secateurs to cut the flowers. Back in the early years of the century it was recommended that "they ought not to be cut with either scissors or a knife, but by a sharp, quick upward pull the whole stem comes away from the axil of the leaf in which it grows; or the picker can seize the stalk quite at the base, and with a sharp side movement and upward pull, done quickly, take it clean away". Well, I tried it and it was, how shall I say, unsuccessful. But with practice I am sure it is very quick, especially for commercial growers.

Vase life

When simply taken from the garden and arranged in tap water in a warm room, as we are tempted to do when time is short, sweet peas will only last two or three days. There are, however, ways to prolong their vase life.

The most successful techniques are not available to home gardeners. Deterioration of flowers is caused by a reaction to ethylene gas and commercial florists can use STS (Silver thiosulphite) or MCP gas (correctly 1-MCP: 1-methylcyclopropene) to inhibit the flowers' reaction to ethylene and delay the process. However, in the home a number of techniques have proved useful.

A Japanese researcher, Kazuo Ichimura, writing in the Japan Agricultural Research Quarterly, has shown that vase life can be increased from two and a half days to six days by adding sugar to the water; he used a dilution of 100g per litre/1lb per gallon. (Incidentally, when this followed a treatment with STS, vase life was extended to almost nine days.) At first this may seem particularly impressive when you consider that his flowers were kept at a constant temperature of 23°C/75°F, far higher and more constant than in a domestic environment. But in fact a high-temperature, constantly-lit environment has been recommended by others.

This approach is paralleled by a number of growers. One suggests mixing two parts water with one part of lemon-lime soda (not the diet version), which creates the effect of a low-pH, high-sugar solution. Using de-ionized water at a very low pH, 3.5, has been recommended by Dr John N. Sacalis of Rutgers University in New Jersey.

With sweet peas responding so adversely to ethylene, it is advisable to keep them away from fruit bowls, especially bananas, and from other flowers (which also generate ethylene). Keep them in a breezy place where the ethylene that the flowers themselves produce will be dispersed quickly.

It has also been suggested that flowers be moved overnight to an environment with a temperature of 22°C/72°F and kept in good light, in particular "cool white" fluorescent lamps. Many people also recommend recutting the stem, under water if possible, after a couple of days to help prolong life.

Pollen beetle

There was a time when pollen beetle was an infuriating pest. This small black creature was found, sometimes in unexpected numbers, in the keel of sweet pea flowers from where it would emerge to move around the flowers after arranging in the house or staging for exhibition. It is generally recognized that the sudden upsurge in this irritating, rather than damaging, pest coincided with the dramatic increase in the planting of oil seed rape.

In recent years it seems to have been on the wane, but there is also a way of reducing its impact. After cutting the flowers, stand them in a relatively dark place such as at the back of a garage, with one good source of outdoor natural light at the other end. The pollen beetles will soon leave the flowers and move towards the light.

Weddings and anniversaries

Sweet peas are popular flowers for weddings, partly because of their scent but also because among their vast range of colours there are usually many which will harmonize well with the dress colours of the bride and bridesmaids. But it is important not to leave the actual cutting until the day of the event: being taken from the bright, airy and warm garden to a cool and relatively dark room (like a church) will stop the flowers opening. Cut them the day before and they will have time to settle and develop their poise and fragrance.

There are many appropriate-sounding sweet peas, including a number with celebratory names, and also many with women's first names, which could be used in wedding bouquets. There are no sweet peas with men's first names, only some combined with surnames.

Celebratory names

'Balcony Bride'
'Blushing Bride'
'Celebration'
'Honeymoon'
'Wedding Day'

For women

'Annabelle'
'Bobby's Girl'
'Bridget'
'Carlotta'
'Charlie's Angel'
'Claire Elizabeth'
'Corinne'
'Daphne'
'Dawn'
'Diana'
'Ella'
'Emma'
'Fatima'
'Fiona'
'Gwendoline'
'Imogen'
'Jilly'
'Juliet'
'Lizbeth'
'Louise'
'Lucy'
'Margot'
'Marion'
'Pamela'
'Phoebe'
'Rosalind'
'Sarah'
'Sonia'
'Sophie'
'Sylvia'

Other suitable names

'Avon Beauty'
'Beauty Queen'
'Evening Glow'
'Lavender Bridesmaid'
'Lovely Lady'
'Moorland Beauty'
'Ruby Anniversary'
'Valentine'

In a patio situation, using fine black plastic mesh as support for sweet peas allows a view of both the flowers and the garden in the distance.

Chapter Fourteen
The basics of exhibiting

Exhibiting sweet peas is not my speciality; in fact I've never in my life staged an exhibit of sweet peas. Still, as this book is intended more for gardeners than exhibitors, perhaps this is not a disaster. I have, however, seen many fine exhibits and what I must highlight in this chapter is the difference between growing sweet peas simply for enhancing the garden or for cutting for the house, and growing them for exhibition.

Exhibition standards are rigorous. The regulations governing exhibiting and judging of exhibits, issued each year by National Sweet Pea Society, run to 30 sections. In addition each show has its own 'schedule' – a set of rules which lay out what can be entered in which class: how many vases, how many stems in each vase, permissible varieties and so on. Time and effort can be entirely wasted by not ensuring that your exhibit is staged in accordance with the schedule; a mistake can lead to the dreaded NTS: your exhibit will not be judged, being Not To Schedule.

A spectacular bowl of 'Mrs Bernard Jones' on an exhibit from Matthewmans Sweet Peas at the Chelsea Flower Show. This is an entirely different way of staging sweet peas compared with competitive exhibition.

MRS BERNARD JONES

There are four stages in the process of exhibiting: choosing the appropriate varieties; growing the plants; cutting and transporting the flowers to the show; staging the exhibit.

Choosing varieties

Some varieties more than others tend to develop the characteristics required at shows, so it is not a matter simply of growing a range of colours. The Annual of the National Sweet Pea Society publishes audits of the previous year's shows in which the varieties which have been entered most often, and won the most prizes, are set out. Start with varieties which are on these lists, and preferably those near the top.

The splendid Centenary Celebration book of the NSPS aggregated all the annual statistics for their shows over the last century and listed the most successful varieties by decade. For the 1990s the top ten varieties were, in order: 'Jilly', 'Anniversary', 'White Supreme', 'Nora Holman', 'Charlie's Angel', 'Angela Ann', 'Restormel', 'Mrs Bernard Jones', 'Honeymoon' and 'Eclipse'.

The list for the 1980s is very different, and included only two of those in the top ten for the 1990s, 'Mrs Bernard Jones' and 'Honeymoon'. The top variety in the 1980s, 'Royal Wedding', did not feature in the 1990s top ten having been superseded by 'White Supreme'. Only 'Honeymoon', still well-placed in the 1990s, was also well placed in the 1970s. This proves two things: fashions change, and/or, from the exhibitors' point of view at least, improved varieties of sweet peas are still being introduced. Either way, while this list is certainly a good current guide to the best show varieties, be aware of those that are currently succeeding and check the audits for the various shows.

Keep in mind, even when ordering seed, the classes which you intend to enter as some require a specific number of distinct varieties; always grow a few extra varieties to allow leeway in choice as the show approaches.

Growing the plants

Plants for showing must be grown on the cordon system (page 108): growing naturally will not produce the long stems, large flowers and good place-ment required by judges and so the space, and the time, must be set aside. The aim is produce enough fine stems of flowers to meet the requirements of the class in the show which you expect to enter.

Bernard Jones, in his fine book *The Complete Guide to Sweet Peas*, published throughout the 1960s, 70s and 80s, defines "the perfect show bloom" as follows in his 1975 edition:

> "The ideal spike is composed of four or five blooms, neatly spaced on a stiff wiry stem, not coarse and fleshy, anything from say seventeen to twenty or more inches overall; blooms should alternate in orderly sequence down the stem, without either undue gap or bunched effect. Size of bloom, termed 'weight', is of course an advantage, and each bloom should have perfect formation – a broad standard or back petal, well spread out, and without hint of either hooding or undue reflex, that is, folding back each side; two wings, not too close together and yet not spread out too widely; and between them a keel enclosing the reproductive assembly."

When you realize that a single entry may require three vases, each containing 12 stems, each with four flowers at their best and shaped to perfection, that's 144 individually perfect flowers, arranged symmetrically on their stems, just for one entry to one show. The most prestigious class of all, The Daily Mail Cup at the National show, requires vases of 12 different varieties, each containing up to 15 stems. And if a stem has five flowers, the lowest of which is past its best, nipping it off will not fool the judges.

Fortunately, sweet pea classes at local shows are less demanding. For the newcomer to exhibiting, the wisest way to start is to visit the major shows and to make a careful inspection of the entrants, especially the winners, combined with entering shows yourself at a more modest level. Talk to experienced exhibitors at shows; ask them to discuss with you the merits and de-merits of the exhibits; try to get them to invite you to see how they grow their plants! And, of course, join the NSPS, Scottish

National Sweet Pea, Rose and Carnation Society and your local sweet pea society if there is one.

Be aware that the spectacular commercial exhibits staged at Chelsea and other major flower shows, while startlingly impressive in themselves, are not staged in the same way as is required at competitive shows.

Cutting and transporting the flowers

Cut blooms about 24 hours before they are to be judged, with the top flower open but perhaps still a little smaller than the others showing that it is young and fresh; it will open fully by judging time. The lowest flower should also still be in its prime.

Immediately they are cut, put them into water as this reduces stress, keeps them fresh and helps prevent callusing of the base of the shoot which will inhibit water uptake later. Take them into a cool, bright place indoors and leave them in water for about three hours.

For a local show, remove the blooms from water and wipe the stems with kitchen paper (take care, for some brands will leave white fluff on the stems). Stand them in a bucket close enough to support each other yet not be squashed; they can then be loaded into the car for the journey.

For longer journeys, packing flat in the boxes used by florists works well. Stems can be laid out in rows, one row of flowers alongside the other with stems lined up along the length of the box, and protected by a layer of kitchen paper which will also soak up any water splashes. With flowers at both ends of the box a surprising number can be packed without damage. They will keep for many hours in this condition.

Staging

This is an art, instruction on which it is difficult to give in a few sentences; there is nothing better than watching an expert at work but very detailed advice is also given in the invaluable book by Bernard Jones, which includes a great deal of advice based on his many years of successful showing.

There are, however, some simple precautions which should be kept in mind to prevent disaster. Most shows require you to enter in advance, so make sure you do this by the closing date; you cannot just turn up. When you arrive at the venue, if you feel that you do not have enough quality flowers for the class which you originally entered, you cannot simply change class at the last minute. And if this realization comes to you a few days before the show, be courteous enough to cancel. Double check that your vases of flowers, and your entry generally, is in accordance with the schedule; if in doubt, check with the show secretary.

And what can you win? More respect than cash it has to be said, although many national awards also come with a trophy which you can retain for the year.

Chapter Fifteen
Sweet peas in the United States

It is a common misconception that sweet peas are impossible to grow in the United States. This, I have to confess, is often claimed by the British who like to think that they're the best at everything horticultural. And it's certainly true that British gardeners grow some very fine sweet peas. It is also the case that apart from mixed packets in the big stores, few American retailers now stock the types best suited to summer heat, and rarely in separate colours. Stocks have also deteriorated so that unless seed is bought from a specialist (page 137), gardeners may be disappointed despite having tried to do the right thing. Yet wild sweet peas are native to Sicily whose Mediterranean climate is matched more closely in some parts of the United States than in the relatively uniform cool British conditions; appreciating the way they grow naturally in the Med educates us on to how to grow them here (page 98).

Unlike Britain where the same varieties and much the same growing techniques can be applied almost anywhere, in the United States climatic conditions vary in different parts of the country – and even in a single state – so much so that different varieties and techniques are required in different areas. If sweet peas remain difficult to grow after reviewing what follows, contact your state horticultural extension service, local Master Gardeners and local societies, call the experts on your local radio phone-in shows or write to the gardening columnists in your local newspapers for advice specific to your area.

One problem that sometimes faces American gardeners is that sweet pea seed imported from Britain is often treated, as a precaution against the introduction of pests. Unfortunately, this can dramatically reduce germination. If you find your seed germinates unexpectedly badly, contact your supplier.

California

California is an enormous state, with many climates, and it is not possible to recommend a single approach. But it is encouraging that, until relatively recently, much of the world's sweet pea seed was produced in California so it is indeed possible for sweet peas to flourish. The Cupid types probably do better in California than anywhere else.

In general, California-grown sweet peas will flower most reliably from winter to early spring, depending upon the zone. The best advice is to sow in August or September (this applies to the mild-winter areas, Sunset zones 12, 13, 17, 21, 22, 23, 24); choose Cuthbertsons (which require 11 hours of daylight to flower) and other "early" or "winter-flowering" types like 'Winter Elegance' (which require 10 hours of daylight) for flowering as early as late December or January to early spring. Spencer types (needing 12 hours) also can be grown in this way but will flower later. In Sunset zones 7, 8, 9, 12–24, you can also plant from October to early January. Everywhere else, you can plant the early types from February. The key is to try to ensure that they are flowering in the two months before summer heat becomes overpowering. Seed can be sown where it is to flower, or can be sown in pots six to eight weeks before you plan to plant out. Water with a liquid feed before planting, and afterwards, and consider a little temporary shade if necessary.

In areas where the fall is hot and dry, the provision of moisture is crucial and starting in pots is often more convenient. Alternatively, wait until November, or later, when valuable rainfall is more likely but flowering will be later.

For flowering in summer, depending upon the zone, seed can also be sown from November to January. Sweet peas will thrive in summer temperatures of up to 26°C/80°F, but will suffer badly as the temperature climbs further; they also hate hot, dry winds. The Cuthbertsons and other early or winter-flowering types will flower first, but the old-fashioned Grandiflora types are unusually heat-resistant, being closer to their Mediterranean ancestors than the modern Spencer types. From the point of view of Californian and other Southern gardeners, the Spencers have the disadvantage of being bred, almost without exception, in the British climate. They may have the largest blooms and the widest range of colours, but they bloom about three weeks after the Grandifloras and are least tolerant of fierce conditions. So, in the warmest zones of southern California, while the "early" varieties can be sown in October or November for spring flowering, the later-flowering Spencer types tend to grow slowly and then, as they pick up in April, the sudden onset of hot weather ruins them before they have a chance to flower.

In coastal areas in the northern parts of the state, and at high altitude, where summers are cooler, Spencers and Grandifloras can be sown in October or November for early summer flowering, or again in March for summer bloom. In the Bay area, where the climate is less uncomfortable for sweet peas, it is possible to sow in late spring for flowering in September and October.

In hot-summer areas, flowering can be prolonged by planting in sites where there is some protection from the sun for part of the day. In areas with cooler summers, exposure to full light promotes the best growth, but where the heat is overpowering to the plants, the best flower colour and the most prolific flowering requires a little dappled overhead shade.

It is also perhaps wise, when plants will be forced to tolerate some heat, to avoid those varieties in the scarlet and orange range which are less tolerant of hot sun.

Texas and Florida

In the hotter lowland areas, sowing in September and October for flowering in spring, before the fiercest summer heat, is ideal. Be sure to keep the seed constantly moist; again, sowing in pots can make this necessity less troublesome. As in California, Cuthbertsons, Grandifloras, and winter-flowering types will all succeed; the problem with the Spencer types is that their longer growing season prevents their blooming period running its course before being cut short by the ferocity of summer.

In cooler, often higher, areas, fall sowing will work well but sowing in early spring is also effective. Here Spencers are more likely to be successful.

Other southern states

Sowing from November to January usually works well; remember that the seed germinates most quickly and completely in a temperature of not less than 10°C/50°F and must be kept moist. Again, it is often most convenient to raise the plants in pots and transplant to their growing positions about six weeks later.

Midwest

The problem in this region is the abrupt transition from winter to summer with but a short spring. Sowing in pots in February or March is usually necessary as the plants need to become well established and in flower before the summer heat becomes too oppressive. The protection of a sun room will allow an early start at a time when outside temperatures are too cold for sowing. Waiting until the soil temperature is sufficiently high and sowing outside, usually in April, will not allow enough time for the plants to mature and flower before being debilitated by the heat. Cuthbertsons and Grandiflora types will tolerate the heat better than other types. The dwarf Cupid type, which also seems unusually heat-resistant, would also be worth trying especially in containers where watering can be more easily continued.

Pacific Northwest

Although in some areas the most suitable for Spencer sweet peas, owing to the similarity of its climate to Britain where the Spencers were developed, this region still varies sufficiently to require different approaches in different areas.

Around Seattle and the Puget Sound area, Portland and the Willamette valley, and the coastal areas of Washington and Oregon (Sunset zones 5 and 6) there is a mild, marine-type climate and gardeners can generally follow the British model of sowing in the fall for early summer colour or, as most gardeners in the area do, sow in early spring for summer flowering. Spring sowing can be made direct into the soil or in pots on heating pads for planting out in early April.

In southern Oregon away from the coast, in central and eastern Oregon and Washington, and in all of Idaho (Sunset zone 1) the summer climate is different with hot days and cool nights (sometimes even freezing in mid-July) and with little rain. Growing sweet peas here is especially challenging and spring-sowing Cuthbertsons, Winter Elegance and Grandifloras is most likely to be successful.

Northeast

The cold winters and hot summers, either individually or together, are the limiting factors in this area and provide the most difficult of conditions in which to grow sweet peas. Sowing outdoors is unlikely to be successful as even sweet peas, which are tough as annuals go, cannot stand the low winter temperatures of USDA zone 7 and below.

Sowing in February, March or April, in pots either indoors or in the sun room from which the worst of the frost can be excluded, is the best way to start. Gauge your sowing time by working back from the approximate last frost date in your area – plant out six weeks before your last frost date, and therefore sow the seed six to eight weeks before that.

Having said that, G. W. Kerr has some interesting observations on fall planting in *Sweet Peas Up-to-Date*, published by Burpee near Philadelphia (USDA zone 6):

"Our experiments at Fordhook Farms have shown that Sweet Peas sown in early October made growth about three inches tall before severe weather set in, and that subsequently the plants were frozen out, while seed sown in November and early December just started to germinate before frost, and as there were no top growths to freeze, withstood winter and started away strongly with the first mild weather in March, the earlier varieties showing flower on May 15th, while the ordinary varieties of Grandiflora and Spencer types were in full bloom in early June."

Trials at Cornell University, at Ithaca, New York (USDA zone 5), in 1909 prove without doubt that for Grandifloras and the new Spencers, fall planting produced earlier flowers the following year. As it happens, two varieties still grown today were used in their trials. Eighty-two per cent of the seeds of the Grandiflora 'King Edward VII', sown in the open ground, when the soil was quoted as being "excellent" on 10 November, germinated, and first flowered on 19 June. The first comparable germination in spring, a sowing on 22 March, flowered on 27 June. Seventy-two per cent of the seeds of 'Countess Spencer' sown on the same November day germinated, their first flowers appearing on 20 June. From the 22 March sowing, flowers opened on 1 July.

Echoing Kerr's remarks, Alvin C. Beal who ran the trial wrote: "In all these trials there was no top growth, but some plants of the first two sowings (on October 20 and 30) were just piercing the surface, when winter set in. The third planting (November 10) germinated but the last two (November 20 and 30) did not appear above the surface of the ground until the following April." Far fewer seeds of these last two sowings germinated, but those that did flowered with the earlier sowings. He concludes: "The results indicate that the planting should be delayed as late as is practicable, but not so late that the seed must be sown in a cold, wet, heavy soil."

I was astonished and delighted when I read this – that autumn sowing of sweet peas, in the open ground, can be very successful as cold as USDA zone 5. You heard it here, nearly 100 years after it was first reported!

Appendix I

AWARDS TO SWEET PEAS

This is all something of a minefield. The Royal Horticultural Society's awards, made jointly with the National Sweet Pea Society, after trial at the RHS gardens at Wisley in Surrey, are the most prestigious awards. Under the current scheme, plants of potential new introductions and, for comparison, of established varieties, are grown at Wisley, both naturally and, where appropriate, on cordons. The trials are grown with great skill by the Wisley staff and, as well as being assessed by the judging committee with awards in mind, also provide a spectacle which visitors can enjoy for much of the summer.

The Award of Garden Merit is the premier award. The RHS regulations state that every AGM plant should be of outstanding excellence for garden decoration or use, be available in the trade, be of good constitution and require neither highly specialist growing conditions or care. Considering that there are actually very few poor sweet peas available today, those awarded an AGM are indeed outstanding varieties. Look for the familiar AGM cup symbol in catalogues and on seed packets.

Today, the AGM is awarded after assessment at the trials but, when first instituted, the system was launched by a few awards being given "round the table", by a committee of experts taking into account awards under the old system.

The question of "availability" is a tricky one. In 2000, AGMs were given to four varieties "subject to availability"; they were not available at the time the award was made, but it was expected that they would be made available in the near future; when they are seen to be listed, the award can be confirmed. In the same way, when a variety which has been awarded an AGM ceases to become available, perhaps because it has been superseded or because a seed company closes down, it should lose its AGM. There is a formal procedure for removing the award from those varieties no longer available.

Under the previous system, before it was streamlined and improved, varieties were eligible to be Commended, Highly Commended, awarded an Award of Merit, or (the top award) a First Class Certificate. In the listings that follow, I have included awards back to and including 1970 so they cover both systems.

Awards are also given 'for exhibition' and here a variation of the old arrangement continues,

The sweet pea trial at the RHS Gardens at Wisley in Surrey, with Intermediate varieties in front and Spencers behind.

although the categories of Highly Commended and Commended were replaced by a single award, Preliminary Commendation. This is altogether a slightly ambiguous award as it is not based on show results or even appearance in a vase; the varieties are judged at the trial as exhibition varieties. This award seems of little value, for although exhibitors can find a clue as to how new introductions might perform on the showbench, the "new seedling" classes at shows will often provide a better guide. The audits of winning varieties at shows, produced each year by the NSPS, seem a far more useful guide to the best show varieties; I have therefore not listed them.

A different range of awards is given after trial at what is now the RHS garden at Harlow Carr at Harrogate in Yorkshire (previously the garden of the Northern Horticultural Society) and another range is given at trials of the Scottish National Sweet Pea, Carnation and Rose Society in Glasgow.

Awards are also noted on the descriptions of individual varieties.

Awards of Garden Merit (AGM)

This list is given irrespective of availability, as recent varieties that were unavailable at the time of writing may soon be so.

'Alaska Blue' 2000
'America' 1995
'Apricot Queen' 1994
'Aunt Jane' 1997
'Bert Boucher' 1997
'Bishop Rock' 1994
'Bobby's Girl' 2000
'Borderline' 1994
'Bristol' 1999
'Charlie's Angel' 1993
'Colin Unwin' 1994
'Dave Thomas' 1997
'Dawn Chorus' 1997
'Dorothy Eckford' 1995
'Elinor' 1996
'Evening Glow' 1996
'Explorer Mixed' 1994

'Flora Norton' 1995
'Florencecourt' 1999
'Geniana' 2000
'Gwendoline' 1998
'Hannah's Harmony' 1996
'Janet Scott' 1995
'Jayne Amanda' 1994
'Jilly' 1994
'King Edward VII' 1995
'Kiri Te Kanawa' 1997
'Knee-Hi' (Bodger) 2000
'Lizbeth' 1999
'Margaret Joyce' 1997
'Marie's Melody' 1996
'Marmalade Skies' 1994
'Millennium' 1997
'Mrs Bernard Jones' 1994
'Noel Sutton' 1994
'Oban Bay' 1997
'Oklahoma' 2000
'Patio Mixed' 1996
'Patricia Anne' 1999
'Phoebe' 1997
'Pink Cupid' 1995
'Pinocchio' 1999
'Pocahontas' 1996
'Ron Entwistle' 1999
'Sicilian Pink' 1995
'Solway Fanfare' 1996
'Southbourne' 1994
'Starlight Sonata' 2000
'Tahiti Sunrise' 1996
'Teresa Maureen' 1996
'Toby Robinson' 1994
'Vera' 2000
'Virgo' 1999
'White Supreme' 1994

First Class Certificate (FCC)

'Charlie's Angel' 1987
'Fergie' 1986
'Lady Diana' 1981
'Madrid' (Jet Set Series) 1972
'Monte Carlo' (Jet Set Series) 1972

A 'Mrs Bernard Jones'
B 'Millennium'
C 'Jilly'
D 'Noel Sutton'
E 'Evening Glow'
F 'Oklahoma'
G 'Dave Thomas'
H 'Gwendoline'

'Naples' (Jet Set Series) 1972
'Westminster' (Jet Set Series) 1972

Award of Merit (AM)

'Amsterdam' (Jet Set Series) 1972
'Anne Sutton' 1974
'Blue Elf' 1977
'Blue Triumph' 1974
'Bristol Cream' 1989
'Crimson Elf' 1977
'Daniel Thomas' 1978
'Desdemona' 1977
'Elisabeth Collins' 1972
'Ellen' 1973
'Fascination' 1989
'Firebird' 1989
'Flying Visit' 1978
'Goya' 1975
'Grace of Monaco' 1981
'Helen' 1986
'Helen Thomas' 1986
'Ivory Queen' 1985
'Jack Bridger' 1977
'Juliet' 1977
'Karen Tremewan' 1981
'Lavender Lassie' 1984
'Lilac Elf' 1977
'Maggie May' 1974
'Maroon Elf' 1977
'Mollie Rilstone' 1991
'Nancy Colledge' 1977
'Navy Elf' 1977
'Nimrod' 1975
'North Shore' 1983
'Pandora' 1973
'Pink Elf' 1977
'Red Ensign' 1974
'Rosalind' 1977
'Sally Ann' 1991
'Salmon Elf' 1977
'Southampton' 1975
'Summer Star' 1973
'Tivoli' 1977
'Vienna' (Jet Set Series) 1972
'White Elf' 1977

'Wiltshire Ripple' 1982
'Xenia Field' 1973
'Yasmin Khan' 1991

Highly Commended (HC)

'Aerospace' 1982
'Alan Titchmarsh' 1985
'Alison Elizabeth' 1986
'Amigo' 1971
'Angela Ann' 1984
'Arbor Low' 1983
'Astronaut' 1989
'Avon' 1978
'Bert Boucher' 1988
'Beryl's Jewel' 1990
'Bianca' 1977
'Bleaklow' 1981
'Blue Ice' 1983
'Blue Mist' 1978
'Blue Pearl' 1984
'Brenda Bridger' 1982
'Bridget' 1988
'Caroline' 1978
'Chris' 1978
'Christchurch Rose' 1983
'Claire' 1980
'Colin Unwin' 1984
'Corinne' 1974
'Cream Beauty' 1972
'Cream Elf' 1976
'Curbar Edge' 1984
'Denis Compton' 1987
'Denise' 1984
'Derry Scarlet' 1991
'Desdemona' 1976
'Doctor' 1975
'Emily' 1987
'Ena Margaret' 1974
'Enterprise' 1975
'Explorer Crimson' 1991
'Explorer Mid-Blue' 1991
'Explorer Rose Pink' 1991
'Explorer Scarlet' 1991
'Fair Charm' 1971
'Firecrest' 1986

'Fred Burfoot' 1974
'Garden Party' 1985
'Georgina' 1975
'Hard Times' 1987
'Honeypink' 1978
'Jacqueline' 1987
'Joanne' 1980
'Josephine Williams' 1983
'Juliana' 1980
'Julie' 1980
'Julie Margaret' 1983
'Juliet' 1976
'King's Bride' 1991
'King's Frill' 1991
'Lady Susan' 1991
'Laura' 1988
'Ledston Luck' 1987
'Leonard Montague' 1991
'Lilac Silk' 1987
'Lily Morris' 1972
'Lovely Lady' 1982
'Lynda Jane' 1986
'Lynda's Blush' 1984
'Margaret Wildgoose' 1987
'Maroon Wonder' 1970
'Mary Pannell' 1990
'Melanie Ann' 1990
'Nanette' 1984
'Nora Holman' 1990
'Ophelia' 1977
'Pageantry' 1985
'Pamela' 1990
'Pennine Floss' 1983
'Percy Thrower' 1983
'Persian Carpet' 1972
'Phoebe' 1976
'Phoebe' 1977
'Pink Expression' 1987
'Pink Omega' 1987
'Pretty Lady' 1987
'Pretty Polly' 1991
'Renaissance' 1977
'Restormel' 1986
'Rievaulx Abbey' 1985

'Rosalind' 1970
'Roy Phillips' 1984
'Sarah Jane' 1972
'Scarlet Elf' 1976
'Serene' 1980
'Silvia' 1977
'Sky-Ray' 1975
'Snowdonia Park' 1980
'Snowflake' 1984
'Subtle Charm' 1990
'Sunset' 1987
'Super Star' 1982
'Susan Bristow' 1970
'Tom Bufton' 1984
'Trisha' 1985
'Tweedie' 1981
'Two Tone' 1977
'Wendy' 1987
'White Supreme' 1987
'Yorkshire Ripple' 1990
'Yvonne' 1989
'Zoe' 1983

Commended (C)

'Annie Good' 1978
'Antiquity' 1977
'Blue Lady' 1982
'Bright Dawn' 1982
'Candy Frills' 1975
'Clarice' 1978
'Concorde' 1978
'Ellen Mary' 1982
'Fay Simmonds' 1975
'Karen Reeve' 1980
'Mollie McLean' 1980
'Morning Rose' 1978
'Picador' 1976
'Silvia' 1976
'Sonia' 1982
'Stepping Stone' 1980
'Supersnoop Navy-Blue' 1982
'Supersnoop White' 1982

Appendix II

Where to buy sweet pea seeds

UNITED KINGDOM AND IRELAND

Sweet pea specialists or stockists of an exceptional range

RJ Bolton & Son Bolton's Garden Centre, Wisbech, PE13 2ZS.

S & N Brackley 117 Winslow Road, Wingrave, Aylesbury, Bucks, HP22 4QB

Eagle Nursery Broadmoor Lane, Stowe-by-Chartley, Stafford, ST18 0LD. www.eaglenursery.co.uk

Peter Grayson 34 Glenthorne Close, Brampton, Chesterfield, Derbyshire, S40 3AR

Kings Seeds, Monks Farm, Pantlings Lane, Coggeshall Road, Kelvedon, Essex, CO5 9PG. www.kingsseeds.com

Kirton Sweet Peas North Farm Cottage, 14 Bristol Road, Pawlett, Bridgwater, Somerset, TA6 4RT. www.webtribe.net/p/pawlett/kerton1.htm

Matthewman's Sweet Peas 14 Chariot Way, Thorpe Audlin, Pontefract, West Yorkshire, WF8 3EZ

Owls Acre Sweet Peas Owl's Acre, Kellett Gate, Low Fulney, Spalding, Lincolnshire, PE12 6EJ. www.lathyrus.com

Diane Sewell 'Overdene', 81 Willingham Road, Over, Cambridge, CB4 5PF

Seeds-by-Size 45 Crouchfield, Boxmoor, Hemel Hempstead, Hertfordshire, HP1 1PA. www.seeds-by-size.co.uk

Unwins Seeds Histon, Cambridge, CB4 9SE. www.unwins-mailorder.co.uk

F. A. Woodcock Lawn Road Nurseries, Walmer, Deal, Kent, CT14 7ND

Other seed companies stocking a useful range of sweet peas

Chiltern Seeds Bortree Stile, Ulverston, Cumbria, LA12 7PB. www.chilternseeds.co.uk

Dobies Seeds Long Road, Paignton, Devon, TQ4 7SX. www.dobies.co.uk

D. T. Brown & Co Station Road, Poulton-le-Fylde, Lancashire, FY6 7HX. www.dtbrownseeds.co.uk

Mr Fothergill's Seeds Gazeley Road, Kentford, Newmarket, Suffolk, CB8 7QB. www.mr-fothergills.co.uk

Plants of Distinction Abacus House, Station Yard, Needham Market, Suffolk, IP6 8AS. www.podseeds.co.uk

Suttons Seeds Woodview Road, Paignton, Devon, TQ4 7NG. www.suttons-seeds.co.uk

Thompson & Morgan Seeds Poplar Lane, Ipswich, IP8 3BU. www.thompson-morgan.com

UNITED STATES AND CANADA

Sweet pea specialists

Enchanting Sweet Peas 244 Florence Avenue, Sebastopol, California 95472. www.enchantingsweetpeas.com

Fragrant Garden Nursery P.O. Box 4246, Brookings, OR 97415. www.fragrantgarden.com

Sweet Pea Gardens 614 Surry Road, Surry, Maine 04684. www.sweetpeagardens.com

Other seed companies stocking a useful range of sweet peas

Baker Creek Heirloom Seeds 2278 Baker Creek Road, Mansfield, Missouri 65704. www.rareseeds.com

Hume Seeds P.O. Box 1450, Kent, WA 98035. www.humeseeds.com

Renee's Garden www.reneesgarden.com

Select Seeds 180 Stickney Hill Road, Union, CT 06076. www.selectseeds.com

Shepherd's Seeds 30 Irene Street, Torrington, CT 06790. www.shepherdseeds.com

Swallowtail Garden Seeds 122 Calistoga Road, #178 Santa Rosa, CA 95409. www.swallowtailgardenseeds.com

Thompson & Morgan Seeds P.O. Box 1308, Jackson, NJ 08527. www.thompson-morgan.com

Appendix III

Further information

Societies

National Sweet Pea Society, St Annes, The Hollow, Broughton, Stockbridge, Hampshire, SO20 8BB
Scottish National Sweet Pea, Rose and Carnation Society, 72 West George Street, Coatbridge, Lanarkshire, ML5 2DD

Books

The Complete Guide to Sweet Peas by Bernard Jones (John Gifford). Invaluable for exhibitors, masses of detail. (Out of print.)

Unwins Book of Sweet Peas by Colin Hambidge (Silent Books). Good introduction.
Other books are mainly of historical interest; for a full list go to www.scentedsweetpeas.co.uk

Websites

For a list of useful links and other information go to **www.scentedsweetpeas.co.uk.**
Readers in the United States and Canada can find their hardiness zone by going to **www.gardenweb.com/zones/zip.cgi** or **www.ivillage.com/home/garden/zone/** and entering their zip code.

Rootrainers

For information on Rootrainers contact them at Rootrainers Kersquarter, Kelso, Roxburghshire, TD5 8HH. www.rootrainers.co.uk

'Horizon' sweet peas being grown for their seed in
Tasmania with further seed crops in the distance.

Glossary

AM — Award of Merit (page 135).

Chitting — Soaking the seed and allowing it to start to germinate before sowing (page 101).

Duplex — With an extra, or occasionally two extra, standards.

FCC — First Class Certificate (page 133).

Fixed — A variety which comes true from seed, without rogues.

Flake — (page 37).

Ground — The underlying or background colour of a flower.

HC — Highly Commended.

Hooded — With the standard held forward over the wings and rolled downwards at the edges.

Keel — The part of the flower, under the wings, which contains the sexual parts.

NSPS — National Sweet Pea Society.

Off types — See Rogue.

RHS — Royal Horticultural Society.

Rogue — A plant which does not meet the criteria for a particular variety.

Self — A flower in which both standards and wings are the same colour.

SNSPRCS — Scottish National Sweet Pea, Rose and Carnation Society.

Sport — A genetic variant, and sometimes a valuable breakthrough.

Standard — The upper, often almost vertical, part of the flower.

Stripe — (page 37).

Wings — The two petals making up the lower part of the flower and angled down around the keel.

Wired — With a narrow margin of contrasting colour on the petals.

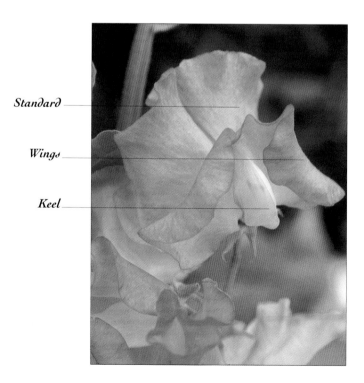

Standard

Wings

Keel

Index of Varieties

The index does not include the alphabetical list in Chapter 7. Page numbers in italic refer to the illustrations. All varieties are *Lathyrus odoratus* unless otherwise indicated.

Acknowledgements

Many people have generously helped me with this book. I'd especially like to thank Martin Thrower, Colin Hambidge, Amanda Smith, Chris Birne, Debbie Breeds and all my friends at Unwins Seeds.

David Kerley, formerly in charge of sweet pea breeding at Unwins, and Dr Keith Hammett have enthusiastically enlightened me as to the peculiarities of sweet pea breeding. Sweet pea breeders David Matthewman, Peter Grayson, Tony Hender and all the sweet pea seed retailers, through their advice, their catalogues or their writings, have been a great help. In the seed trade Tony Byers, Tom Sharples and my friends at Suttons Seeds as well as Keith Sangster, Andrew Tokely, Barrie Sims and my friends at Thompson & Morgan Seeds have, over the years, helped with a wide range of information about sweet peas.

I'd also like to thank Caroline Ball for her help, in particular for editing the National Sweet Pea Society's invaluable Centenary Celebration book and ensuring it is packed with such useful information.

At the Royal Horticultural Society I'd like to thank the many gardeners who have maintained the sweet pea trials so conscientiously since their inception the best part of a hundred years ago and the staff of the trials office who have kept such painstaking records. In particular, I appreciate the generous and friendly assistance of Linda Jones and her current staff.

In the United States I'd especially like to thank Sue Keating of Sweet Pea Gardens, Pat Sherman of Fragrant Garden Nursery, Glenys Johnson of Enchanting Sweet Peas, Gerald Burke, Wayne Winterrowd, David King, and the Mann Library at Cornell University.

My agent Vivien Green and my editors at Batsford, Tina Persaud and Jane Donovan, have been patient, persuasive and professional. Thank you.

Finally, I'd like to thank my wife judywhite – not only for her superb studio plates but for her support during the hurried creation of this book, her wise advice on the text – and for making my life complete by marrying me.

Graham Rice
Log Tavern Lake, Pennsylvania, September 2001